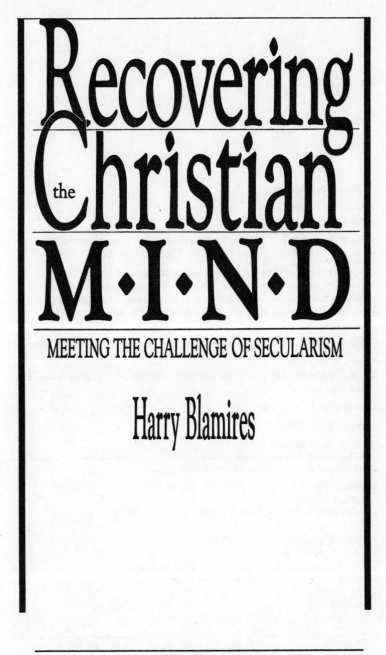

Recovering the Christian MIND

M·I·N·D

MEETING THE CHALLENGE OF SECULARISM

Harry Blamires

INTERVARSITY PRESS
DOWNERS GROVE, ILLINOIS 60515

Published in the United States of America by InterVarsity Press, Downers Grove, Illinois, with permission from MARC, an imprint of Kingsway Publications, England.

InterVarsity Press is the book-publishing division of InterVarsity Christian Fellowship, a student movement active on campus at hundreds of universities, colleges and schools of nursing. For information about local and regional activities, write Public Relations Dept., InterVarsity Christian Fellowship, 6400 Schroeder Rd., P.O. Box 7895, Madison, WI 53707-7895.

Distributed in Canada through InterVarsity Press, 860 Denison St., Unit 3, Markham, Ontario L3R 4H1, Canada.

Unless otherwise noted, Scripture quotations in this publication are from the Holy Bible, King James Version.

Cover illustration: Guy Wolek

ISBN 0-8308-1215-6

Printed in the United States of America

Library of Congress Cataloging in Publication Data

Blamires, Harry.
    [Meat, not milk]
    Recovering the Christian mind/Harry Blamires.
       p.   cm.
    Previously published as: Meat, not milk.
    ISBN 0-8308-1215-6
    1. Theology, Doctrinal—Popular works.   2. Christianity—20th
century.   3. Secularism—Controversial literature.   I. Title.
BT77.B58 1988
230—dc19   87-30979
                                           CIP

17	16	15	14	13	12	11	10	9	8	7	6	5	4	3	2	1
99	98	97	96	95	94	93	92	91	90	89	88					

Acknowledgments

There are one or two paragraphs in this book which have appeared in articles in the *Church Times*. There are more substantial sections where the argument had its origin in lectures delivered at various times and in various places in the United States. In particular, the substance of Chapter 2, 'Our Civilisation and the Fall', owes a great deal to material I originally prepared for the conference of the Christian Legal Society held at Glen Eyrie, Colorado Springs, in 1983. No one who has visited that beautiful area will doubt my sincerity in publicly thanking Lynn Buzzard and the officers of the Christian Legal Society for the opportunity to mix in such wonderful surroundings with such congenial company. It would not be possible for me to recall in how many other places, briefly visited, paragraphs from this and other chapters formed part of lectures and addresses I gave; but when I was involved in 1985 in conducting more sustained summer-school courses at New College, Berkeley, Laity Lodge, Kerrville, Texas, and Regent College, Vancouver, material was certainly used which is found here in print for the first time. For all the happy memories of these occasions my wife and I owe gratitude to our generous hosts, and to none more than to Howard Blake of The Servant Society, in whose car we twice crossed the desert. Nearer home, I am gratefully aware of the benefits that steadily accrue from listening week by week to meaty sermons by Canon Richard Watson from the pulpit of St John's Church, Keswick.

Meat Not Milk

'I have fed you with milk, and not with meat' St Paul wrote in his first epistle to the Corinthians (3:2). He claims to have spoken to them 'as unto babes in Christ' (I Cor 3:1). We think of St Paul's teaching as being emphatically concerned with the conflicting dualities of flesh and spirit, of the fallen state and the state of grace; yet here he introduces a duality of a different kind, not a duality of conflict, but a duality of progress. There is war between flesh and spirit, but the antithesis between milk and meat is an antithesis between two forms of nourishment, one fit for babes and the other fit for grown men and women.

We cannot make sense of adult life with the mental equipment of the child. We cannot afford to carry into adult life a Christian consciousness so under-nourished and anaemic that we slide into accepting faddish convenience recipes for worldly well-being as our daily diet. The evidence is that when the time comes for getting to grips with the Christian faith as adults and not as children, many of our contemporaries abandon their faith. They were early spoon-fed on the milk of the word, but in adulthood they discard the nourishment as babyish, and assume that there is no more to be said. Meanwhile, professing believers, men and women who perhaps make great steps forward in other spheres of life, all too often succumb to the epidemic of *anorexia religiosa* which destroys all appetite for progress in Christian understanding and commitment.

This book attempts to confront the realities of the contemporary scene and to show how full-blooded Christian teaching will bring under judgement much that is taken for granted by people reared on a protein-free Gospel or on no Gospel at all. We have to learn to set life's manifestations of evil and suffering, as well as of goodness and joy, in the context of the divine and human drama which is Christianity's account of what we men and women are here involved in. The Christian worldview is the only integrative counterpoise to a secularism that is decomposing our civilisation. No thoughtful Christian can contemplate and analyse the tensions all about us in both public and private life without sensing the eternal momentousness of the current struggle for the human mind between Christian teaching and materialistic secularism.

1
Our Fallen State

Life's Emergencies

Long ago, an old friend told me a true story which has
proved unforgettable. He had a schoolmaster colleague
in his early teaching days before the War who felt, or pre-
tended to feel, acutely cynical about the perverseness
and contrariness of human experience. He propounded
what he called 'The Law of Maximum Bloodiness' as
being a built-in feature of human life, and when anything went wrong for anybody, he would murmur, 'It's
the Law'. One night during the War he took refuge from
German bombers in an air-raid shelter. The shelter received a direct hit and he was killed. His colleagues recalled his wry slogan, 'It's the Law'. He had become a living example — or rather a dying example — of his own
half-comic, half-serious doctrine. His fate provides an
instance of what we call life's tragic ironies.

Anyone of us could rustle up a dozen instances from
our own experience or from what we read in the press.
There is the family which sets off for its summer holiday,
the car laden with swim-suits, dinghy, picnicking
apparatus, cricket equipment, and the rest. An out-of-
control lorry crashes through the central reservation on
the motorway and the entire family is wiped out in an in-
stant. The newspapers tell us of individuals who suddenly win wealth on the football pools and before long
their seeming good fortune has left a trail of misery in
their lives. And we all have private memories of lives

ironically marred by affliction or disaster.

The schoolmaster who formulated the principle, 'It's the Law', of things going awry presumably thought he was saying something remarkable. His colleagues remembered it as such, a specimen of his wry irony. The ironic force depended on the expectation that the formulation would surprise by its apparent affront to common sense. Do we not feel it more natural for things to go right than for things to go wrong? Is it not more natural for sudden wealth to bring ease and comfort than for it to bring disaster? Is it not more natural for a family holiday to bring refreshment and relaxation than for it to bring calamity?

It all depends. When individual plans went awry and disasters struck between 1939 and 1945, people would say, 'What do you expect? There's a war on'. The situation was regarded as 'exceptional', and normal expectations had to be laid aside. When it was all over, some journalists for several years talked about getting back to 'normalcy'. They apparently meant getting away from shortages and privations, restoring the fabric of bombed cities, setting the wheels of industry turning, and building up the public services for a new age. 'Normalcy' was presumably the converse of 'emergency'. The accepted assumption in wartime was that you might get maimed, killed, or bombed out at any time, your home destroyed, your friends or relations mutilated or killed in action. Peace certainly removed those risks. But has it otherwise established a 'Law' that things now go right? After all, no one would have had any difficulty in finding a job in the 1940s or the 1950s. Do our unemployed youngsters, do our middle-aged workers made redundant — believe that this is a life in which things tend to go right if you do your bit, in which conscientious effort will always bring its reward? Does the young couple on the Social Security register, whose main desire is to marry, build a home, and bring up a family, believe that this is a life in which there is a firm connection between virtue and contentment, between zeal and attainment? Do those who have bought houses and made their homes in villages which the powers-that-be want to use as dumping sites for nuclear waste believe that our peace-time environment is mercifully free of menace?

I live in a beautiful part of the country. Many a picture postcard of the scenes hereabouts suggests peace, tranquillity, and happiness. There are nearby farmsteads, any one of which, if portrayed against the surrounding hills, would stir a spectator with longings to live in such a setting. Yet if I take an afternoon walk, I can within half an hour catch a glimpse of three such idyllic farmsteads, from one of which the young son was killed in a drowning accident, from another of which the son was killed in a car accident, and from the third of which the daughter fell into a swollen river, and her body was swept into the nearby lake. All these are comparatively recent tragedies. And it is only a few weeks ago that I saw a car half buried under a lorry in the road within sight of my window. Firemen cut free the driver of car, but he was dead, a young man with a wife and family expecting him home some 30 miles away. I watched the undertaker arrive to remove the body; and I recalled that the undertaker's own son was killed while riding his motor bike not all that long ago.

In the midst of life we are in death. There may not be a 'Law of Maximum Bloodiness', but there is certainly no 'Law of Optimum Luck'. The 'state of emergency' does not end when war gives place to peace. There is no such civilised condition as that of a state of 'normalcy' freed from the threat of calamity and upheaval. If the wartime blackout kept people imprisoned in their urban homes; the menace of the mugger, the vandal, and the rapist has in the peace-time 1980s the very same effect. Life is an ever-present emergency for all too many of our fellow-creatures.

The Christian Gospel is addressed to men and women whose lives present them with emergencies — with dangers, temptations, demands, threats, and risks. That is only another way of saying that we are fallen creatures living in a fallen world. You can test the validity of any sermon, any theological book, by asking: How far is it addressed to men and women in a state of emergency? If it is not so addressed, then 10 to 1 it is a poor sermon, defective theology. It is no use preaching today to those imaginary people who inhabit the advertisement pages of glossy magazines, whose lives are spent between spick-and-span kitchens and gleaming new motor cars. It is no use preaching to that imaginary family group, father and mother, brother and sister, arm in arm, bright and beautiful, fresh and carefree, who gaze at you from your Access booklet in the hope of persuading you to buy the latest thing in designer shirts. It is no good gearing your theological dicta to that shapely young blonde sipping her coffee in a silk dressing-gown in her Moben kitchen, or to that smart-suited young man caught by the camera midway between the door and the Ford Granada, briefcase in hand. It is no good because plainly none of these people has an aged parent upstairs with Alzheimer's disease or a child in a cot behind the bedroom window with Down's syndrome. None of them has just had cancer diagnosed, or even a hole in the heart. We may overlook the fact that the sky suggests California rather than an English suburb. Look at the garden, how trim and colourful it is. Somehow we can swear that there is not even a coal-mine — let alone a nuclear power station — for miles around.

A package arrived by this morning's mail which suggests that I myself have still one more chance to join this happy throng. It tells me that even in old age and in the presence of illness, the smooth tenor of my worldly ways need not be gravely interfered with — that is provided I subscribe monthly to an insurance that will protect me from the horrors and procrastinations of the National Health Service. To judge from the full-colour picture which conveys the message of my would-be benefactors, illness in old age will only mean reclining comfortably, rosy-faced, in a neatly-made bed, a pamphlet in my hands, a window open to the sunshine, and a charming nurse leaning in my direction with all the time in the world on her hands to attend to my needs. Moreover, my wife sits in an armchair at my bedside with a look so contented that I can only assume the diagnosis to have been confirmed as a common cold without complications. The pamphlet I am studying, by the way, is the table of financial benefits that have accrued from my regular contributions to the insurance company in question.

The picture of life which overlooks or underplays calamity and tragedy would not be worth taking seriously were it not that there is a theology in the air which addresses its imaginary inhabitants instead of addressing real people in a real world. There is a theology which does not speak to human beings in the thick of emergencies, but to human beings moving steadily between birth and death through an equable spring, summer, and autumn of life. It is a theology of speculation and exploration which turns us all into seekers after truth with plenty of time to savour this experience and that, weigh this doctrine and that, until we finally conclude that we may as well make do with the Christian faith. We shall analyse some of the fallacies of this counter-Christianity later in the book. True Christianity does not offer us a theology of speculation and exploration. It offers us a theology of revelation and salvation. And a theology of revelation and salvation is needed because we are fallen creatures living in a fallen world.

When you study the autobiographical records of saintly Christians who have been transported from unbelief to belief, you find that the transition often has an intense and desperate character. Study St Augustine or, in our own age, C S Lewis, in this respect. What is the experience of conversion like? Is it like opening a book one day and saying, 'Ah, now I understand: in future I shall guide my life by these precepts'? It is not. If the men and women of true faith are to be trusted, the relief felt after conversion is the relief of someone who has been saved from drowning, spotted struggling in the sea, winched up on to a helicopter and laid panting there. The convert does not speak as though he has achieved something, mastered some difficult truth at last, solved some problem, attained some new insight. He speaks as one torn from the bowels of destruction by the watchfulness, the care, the unspeakable love of a Saviour. His emotions are of relief, gratitude, and complete self-commitment to the One to whom he owes everything.

Since I wrote the last sentence four hours ago, I have learned of the worries of two affectionate Christian parents who have reason to believe that their 21-year-old son is on drugs. That is the kind of world we inhabit. There is one more case of human weakness that is tearing the heart out of worthy, prayerful believers. No one would know from meeting these two parents that they are not at ease with life in all its aspects. No one would detect what is gnawing at their happiness. But at the level of their spiritual life, their prayer and their meditation, there will be no cover over their worry. They do not try to look God cheerfully in the face as though everything in their garden were lovely. And they do not seek, in answer to their prayer, a word of guidance, a helpful hint on how to get on with young men, a gentle encouraging suggestion that perhaps all may yet come right in the end. They want, in answer to prayer, what every worried or grief-stricken soul wants in answer to prayer — a lifeline thrown out with lifebelts attached, for their son, for themselves.

The Fall and the World Today

Christian teaching, wherever it is sound, wherever it is undiluted by sentimentality, is all about lifelines and lifebelts and not just about good advice and moral uplift. That is because Christian teaching is addressed to fallen men and women in a fallen world. The doctrine of the Fall and the doctrine of original sin are fundamental truths of the most elementary Christian teaching.

Not all Christian truths are of the same category. For that matter, not all scientific truths are of the same category. Some truths, once articulated, are self-evident. Other truths can perhaps only be conveyed by persuasion. For instance, if you wished to explain the law of gravity to a class of schoolchildren, all you would need to do would be to drop a book from your hand to the floor. You might well wish to refer to Isaac Newton and his apple, but the reference to the history of the scientific discovery would not be strictly necessary. On the other hand, if you were anxious to persuade your pupils that, contrary to appearances, the sun does not move round the Earth but the Earth moves round the sun, it would not be enough to point to the sun in the sky and say, 'There you are'. You would probably find it better to set about some historical explanation of how the old Ptolemaic view of the universe which put the Earth at the centre was discredited by the discovery of Copernicus that the sun is the centre of the planetary system and that the Earth and the planets move around it.

In theology there are doctrines which call for some technical argument and historical reference for their explanation. If someone asked you to account for and explain the doctrine of the Trinity, you would no doubt go back to the New Testament to our Lord's insistence that there is one God, that he and the Father are one, and that he will send the Comforter from the Father. It would only be on the basis of such historic reference that you would feel able to elaborate the doctrine of the Trinity in relation to evident human experience. But if you were asked to say what the doctrines of the Fall and of original sin were all about, you would scarcely need to go back to the story of Adam and Eve. You could simply point your finger at the world around: at the way human wickedness causes distress and tragedy, at the way human affairs are arranged so that thousands suffer from famine and poverty in some parts of the world, while vast unwanted food stocks accumulate in other parts of the world, at the fact that the soil is polluted by agricultural technology and the atmosphere by nuclear technology, and at the extravagantly wasteful and damaging use of the earth's reserves of fossil fuel. There may be difficulty for the apologist in conveying some of the great Christian truths persuasively. But surely there can be no difficulty in indicating that human nature has been corrupted so that men and women know full well in their hearts what ought to be done and are imprisoned within economic systems of their own manufacture that prevent them from doing it. How many aged people suffering from cold, perhaps dying of hypothermia, could be rescued from their misery if one return flight by Concorde across the Atlantic were cancelled in favour of using the fuel otherwise?

The doctrine of the Fall of man and the doctrine of original sin are not primarily about what happened in the Garden of Eden in the dawn of history or what happened in the courts of heaven before ever the world was made. These doctrines are about muggers who strike their victims on the London underground at night and rapists who creep up behind their victims in dimly lit alleys; they are about gangs of drunken teenagers who break into the homes of old-age pensioners, bludgeon them, and go off with the meagre contents of their purses; they are about entrepreneurs who intercept foodstuffs destined for famine relief before they reach the starving peasantry and line their pockets with the proceeds on the black market. This is what the doctrine of the Fall is all about: criminal godfathers who make millions while their agents push drugs in Piccadilly, hooking victims and enslaving addicts, and terrorist godfathers who plot the murder of their sectarian enemies in the streets of Belfast or Beirut, widowing their wives and orphaning their children.

You scarcely need to open your Bible to prove that the human race is a race of fallen beings so corrupted by the taint of evil that they know no means of righting what is wrong. On the public scene and in the private domain the situation is the same. We know that it is a wicked world where millions are spent annually on ever more costly and sophisticated means of wiping out the human race. We know that, whatever human brains were created for, it was not that they should be exercised at the highest level of reasoning and the sharpest level of calculation to grapple with the question: How can we further refine this weapon of destruction, how further magnify its capability for extermination? We know that, whatever man ought to be about in brain-work and hand-work, it is not the devising and manufacturing of apparatus for putting an end to human existence and rendering God's Earth uninhabitable. That is the public evidence of the Fall of man. You will not find it in the book of Genesis. You will find it in your daily newspaper.

We are not just arguing that the arms race with all the wealth and effort and all the resources and brain-power it consumes is evidence of the Fall of man. Certainly it is that: it is crying proof of human wickedness. But we are arguing too that it is proof of human powerlessness and proof of the disintegration of man's very nature. For we *know* the arms race is wicked in itself, but we have not the slightest idea in practical terms how we can get from the present international situation to a situation in which such wickedness would be a thing of the past. Persuasive voices, reasoning cogently, convince upright, well-meaning men and women that immense national resources must be assigned to this industry of manufacturing and deploying the machinery of death. The reasoning has moral force. Indeed, we are able to feel virtuous becuase we deprive 'ourselves' of physical benefits to be derived from an improved and more expensive health service so that something called 'Trident' or 'Star Wars', or whatever, shall not be denied its due tribute. Yet when we withdraw in detachment from the area of thought where the pressures of political sloganising bemuse our minds, and ask coolly, reflectively, what we are about in organising missile launchers here and desperate famine there, then we cannot fail to confess to a collective human wickedness of staggering perversity. Perversity, because if we, the human race, are free, as we believe we are, then we, the human race, have chosen the way of bombers rather than of hospital beds in Ethiopia. We have chosen the way of massive arsenals of weapons produced by the ultimate refinements of technological know-how, in place of food in the hands of skeletal African children and roofs over the heads of the sleeping homeless on the streets of Calcutta.

In this respect — in relation to the massive public evidence of the Fall of man — we can, unfortunately perhaps, wriggle away from any sting of conscience, you and I. For you and I can do precious little about it. Voting for this particular party or for that is certainly not going to produce any fundamental change in the world situation in this respect. Even in respect of closer, and seemingly more personal problems such as that of unemployment, there appears to be little that we can do. Yet here again the same situation obtains, for we know in our hearts that only an economic system perversely designed could produce a civilisation like ours. All around us is evidence of things that need to be done in order to cleanse and beautify our environment, in order to care more effectively for the needy and the afflicted, and yet we pay millions of people to do nothing. A civilisation which keeps people idle when there is so much desirable, even necessary work to do, stands under moral judgement. Once again we know that it is wrong, and yet we do not know what to do about it. As something called

'Trident' requires us to spend vast sums of money on it which we would rather use for something else, so something called 'Sterling M3' or 'Monetary Policy' or 'Market Forces' requires us to save on wages for paid work and devote the money to keep workers doing nothing. And if some outraged reader here protests that I am now making 'political' points, I should reply that in my capacity as apologist and expounder I am simply explaining and proving that man is fallen and his civilisation is corrupt.

It would be interesting to speculate how a great poet might write today if he were required to follow the example of Milton and compose a 'Paradise Lost'. He might have great difficulty in picturing heaven, but surely, like Milton himself, he could with relish and insight picture and people hell. He would not have far to seek in search of local colour. Some of his leading characters, the dominant devils, would be easy to name and describe: 'Trident', bristling with weapons like Milton's Moloch, 'Sterling M3', as fat and greasy and pampered as Milton's Belial, and 'Market Forces', a brood of deformed creatures creeping in and out of the womb of Industry like the progeny of Milton's Sin. It is to these idols that we fall down in worship. It is in the name and service of these grotesque, disfigured divinities that we order the lives of fellow human beings. Let the armies of the workless arise and proclaim, 'Blessed be the name of Sterling M3'. Let the hungry and cold, the sick and deprived, assemble together and sing the praise of Trident: 'We have offered you our sacrifice, O Trident — or at least someone has kindly offered it on our behalf. Protect us through the long night watches. Save us waking; guard us sleeping.'

Evidence of the Fall is no less widespread in areas of

life where individual wills are more directly operative
in choosing the way of evil. This lunch-time's news bul-
letin announces that five dead bodies discovered in a
burnt-out house in the New Forest had all been strangled. The murder of one person is as much murder as the
murder of five; but when the victims are multiplied the
mind reels and boggles. A man is charged with murder-
ing seven aged people, each living in solitude. We shud-
der with a peculiar kind of discomfort. Yet surely there
can be no crime worse than the brutal beating to death of
a single victim. Why does the repetition affect us so
sharply? It is because repetition is essentially a feature of
the unremarkable. A string of five murders, or seven
murders, brings the additional enormity that the 'exceptional' nature of the brutal crime is weakened. We do not
want murder 'cheapened' by repetition. We do not want
murder reduced by sheer frequency to the same status as
our daily milk deliveries.

We cannot, of course, define the fallen nature of mankind simply in terms of sensational crimes headlined in
the press. The present reader of this book, I imagine, has
neither a murder nor a rape on his conscience, has never
beaten up an old-age pensioner, nor joined in an escap-
ade to cart gold bullion away illicitly by night from the
warehouses at Heathrow Airport. We who read religious
books must be wary of locating the marks of the fallen
condition in the lives of publicly acknowledged crimi-
nals from whom it may be easy for us to dissociate ourselves. We are not of their company, we can say. Men
who have done time are not of *our* circle. We operate at
a lower level of illegality than they. We take fewer risks.
But we have our Lord's word for it that in so far as we
hate or lust, we have committed murder and adultery in
our hearts and can be properly classed with those who

go the whole hog.

It is not the purpose of this chapter, however, to touch the conscience. The writer has no authority to disseminate guilt. The purpose of this chapter is to argue a case: that we are fallen creatures living in a fallen world. If the case can be made more vividly and more convincingly by pointing to the violence and criminality rampant in our day, so be it. It is the preacher's business to warn us — readers and writer alike — that to project an image of corrupted humanity by focusing on what other people have done is likely to be as perilous spiritually as it is misleading dialectically.

When we look up 'The Fall' in a theological encyclopaedia, we find much about Adam and Eve and the Garden of Eden. But we know in our hearts that the doctrine of the Fall cannot be comfortably written off as a question of something that happened in far-off history or pre-history; accepted or dismissed as a matter of a serpent and an apple, plucked fruit and sewn fig-leaves. We do not have to seek evidence of man's fallen condition by research into the primitive past. We do not even have to seek evidence of man's fallen condition by pricking up our ears when news bulletins record the crimes and follies of people we are never likely to meet. The evidence is here in the writer's own neighbourhood and there in the reader's. It is here in the fact that soon after I came to live here, someone whispered darkly into my ear that Mrs X writes poison-pen letters, while every contact with Mrs X has convinced me that she is quite above any such malignity. It is here in Mrs Wetherup's complaint that Lord Brass lets his deer browse on the very pastures she rents from him for her cattle. It is here in Mr Rigid's attempt to fence off a much-relished section of lake-side land for his private enjoyment. It is here in the fact that

Mr Modest is refused permission to attach a harmless new porch to his little home for fear it should deface an unspoilt valley, while Mr Pocketful is mysteriously permitted to erect a monstrosity in a already over-crowded street. It is here in Mr Landlord's refusal to mend the leaky roof over a lone, frail octogenarian's head, so that she has to put a bucket on the carpet when the rain falls. It is here in the sneering, snarling letters with which a local politician castigates the monstrous iniquities of his party's opponents in the weekly press.

Now you, reader, have a perfect right to add that evidence of the Fall is even more obvious in the thoroughness with which the present writer has observed the failings of others and the relish with which he has recorded them. By doing so, of course, you merely add weight to my argument. You cannot criticise me morally without corroborating me dialectically. On the public scene and on the private scene, we human beings manifest our fallen state every day of our lives.

Facing the Facts of the Fall

There are, of course, other explanations of the causes of life's evils than are embodied in the Christian doctrine of the Fall. Evolutionists trace back the roots of unsocial behaviour in racial history; and we shall have something to say about this reasoning in the next chapter. Marxists lay the blame on systems of government organised for exploitation rather than for the common good. This case must surely stand or fall by the success of communist states in eradicating evil as they eradicate its supposed causes. The Christian believes that failure by men and women to achieve what they will to achieve, whether in a capitalist or a communist society, is continuing evidence of human inadequacy without divine aid.

Advocates of alternative views on this matter tend to complain that the Christian doctrine of original sin pessimistically underestimates the true quality of human nature. The Christian, however, asserts that there is nothing cynical or pessimistic about insisting that men and women are fallen beings.

The very word 'fall' suggests collapse from a position or status which ought to have been maintained. You cannot have Humpty Dumpty without the wall. And you cannot have Adam and Eve without the Garden of Eden. You remedy a fall only by getting up again, by rising again; and you rise to regain the position you had before the fall. To say that human beings are fallen, therefore, presupposes that they have lost a status and that there is a status to be regained. The lost status is their proper status, their truly 'natural' status. Those who say that the doctrines of the Fall and of original sin underestimate human quality and human potentiality are wide of the mark. These doctrines put the highest possible emphasis upon what men and women in their true, their fully realised nature, ought to be and to do. The emphasis of these doctrines on the sadly perverse and corrupt tendencies at work in our hearts and our lives is the reverse side of the coin which proclaims man the child of God made in the image of his Father.

Anyone who has to listen to a circular saw screaming its way through a tree trunk might well declare it to be the most hateful noise he ever hears. Yet by the strictest aural standards there must surely be even more tortuously displeasing sounds. Suppose a large organ were badly out of tune. Suppose that nevertheless someone insisted on playing a Bach fugue on it. A listener would surely find it more gratingly intolerable than a circular saw. And the more musically accomplished the listener were, the more unpleasant he would find the noise. By comparison, the wailing of the saw might be described as not unmusical. After all, the saw was not manufactured with the specific purpose of making a pleasant noise. But the organ was carefully designed and manufactured with the purpose of making a totally different sound from that which the listener has heard. It was designed to be kept in tune. Moreover, the Bach fugue was specifically intended to be played on an instrument perfectly tuned.

As God's created beings, we are out of tune. The finest organ in the world could get gratingly out of tune if neglected. It would certainly not then be any denigration of the organ's quality and usefulness to declare it out of tune and in need of rectification. And it is certainly no denigration of us men and women in our essential nature to be told that we are out of tune.

Insistence on our fallen state does not then represent a denigration of human quality and potential. Nor does it represent a specific commentary on today's world in particular. A danger for the moralist is that if he makes his point by passing judgement on the civilisation of his day and singles out evils prevalent among his contemporaries, he will be judged to be in love with the past. But the informed Christian has no more illusions about the past then he has about the present. This distinguishes him from the reactionary conservative (with a small 'c') who believes that there is now escalating deterioration in human behaviour and that standards once cherished are being abandoned and betrayed. The Christian is a realist. He does not need to be reminded what social conditions were like in the heyday of Victorian Britain, when church worship, family prayers, and Bible reading were practised by far more people than they are today. Neglect of the poor produced horrific instances of hunger and homelessness, rags and privation, disease and vice in conditions so squalid and insanitary that the mind sickens in reading of it. Few of us would elect to change places with our Victorian forebears. Victorian excesses of cruelty in the bullying of children especially should make us chary of joining too loudly in the current spate of condemnation heaped on our educational system. There are hair-raising accounts in Victorian novels of the agonies brutally inflicted on English children in the age of British imperial splendour. The inhabitants of Victorian England were no less and no more plainly fallen creatures than are the inhabitants of twentieth-century England. Christian doctrine will not allow us to escape from awareness of the true human condition into the notion that what is wrong with us is something that has overtaken us in the last 100 years.

So much secular diagnosis of what is wrong with the world takes one of two escape routes from hard facts. The first escape route is to this notion that we have lost touch with 'old values' and 'old standards' and need to recapture what we have lost in the way of a temporal historic status and possession. The Christian message is not that. It is that we need to recapture what we have lost in the way of an eternal and spiritual endowment. We have lost it, and the Victorians had lost it too. The second escape route from facing up to our fallen condition is to the notion that we are on the way to establishing a just and equitable society where none need want and none need suffer, and with effort we shall get there. It is only a matter of clearing up a few abuses inherited from the past, wiping out the exploiters and the parasites, and we shall attain communal stability and contentment. The

Christian message is not that. No amount of purely human effort is going to remedy the condition of a fallen race. Escape routes by which people flee from human realities into dreamy idealisation of the past or of the future are simply not open to the Christian.

This is a matter with a moral aspect. There is a connection between appeals by advertisers to private acquisitiveness referred to earlier in this chapter and lavish promises of public reform by political action. Both appeals fasten hopes on the future. And in fastening human hopes on the future there is always an element of wanting something we have not got. This is so whether what we look forward to is a better educational system in the public domain or a pleasanter house to live in as a private ambition. It is, of course, quite proper to strive for better things both in public and in private life. But the Christian refuses to indulge in dreamy idealisation of the future as an escape route from facing the realities of the present. We have no more reason to believe that new legislation will rapidly bring public prosperity and abundance than we have to believe the advertisers' promise of future bliss purchased by taking out an insurance policy.

We have to bring common sense to bear on the question of what governments can achieve. Arguments rage in the Western world about privatising a public utility or nationalising a private monopoly, about the propriety of deficit-financing, or about the inflationary risks involved in stimulating an economy in pursuit of growth. Yet we are aware in the back of our minds that what transpires when the debate is settled will not save a single soul and probably not increase the total sum of human happiness at all. We can sympathise today with Swift's King of Brobdingnag in *Gulliver's Travels*, who 'gave it for his opinion that whoever could make two ears of corn, or two blades of grass, to grow upon a spot of ground where only one grew before, would deserve better of mankind, and do more essential service to his country, than the whole race of politicians put together.'[1] Unfortunately, however, we have now created a world where even such patent expressions of wisdom need to be modified. If you can double the ears of corn and blades of grass in one of the Third-world countries, you will certainly benefit the inhabitants. But in civilised Europe, any such multiplication of productivity would be disastrous. The powers-that-be would pay you to desist.

The Christian surely ought not to have exaggerated expectations of what the fallen leaders and legislators of a fallen race can achieve in putting to rights the affairs of souls voyaging through time to eternity. Today's newspaper speaks of a poll conducted among the young and proclaims 'apathy' to be the dominant mood of 18-year-olds to 20-year-olds. If 'apathy' means, as it appears to mean, that these young people are not going to put their trust in political parties to create a heaven on earth, and consider it scarcely material in terms of human welfare whether they vote left or right, then 'apathy' sounds like another word for 'wisdom'. Surely the upheavals of our century have taught us not to put too much trust in political recipes for our ills.

The constitutions of the Western democracies do in fact discourage citizens from putting too much trust in political leaders. The democratic electoral system prevents the permanent possession of power by any individual or any party beyond the period that popular election allows. Why devise such a system? Some people will argue that it is because 'democracy' is a wonderful system of government, giving all people a share in decision making. Is not this at best a half-truth? For how large is the share in decision making that the individual citizen exercises in the span of a lifetime? And does the system necessarily throw up the best leaders? Why, the electors cannot necessarily get their will even in such a small matter as the character of the government or the personality of its leader. Governments rule with minority support and a Prime Minister may hold office with the approval of less than a quarter of the electorate. If this is a wonderful system, one might say, then it speaks ill of human capacity to devise a system at all.

In a way it does. Democracy is a wise system precisely because it speaks ill of human capacity. With all its faults, it is a superbly appropriate system because it faces facts. It faces the fact that power corrupts, that no one can be trusted with too much of it or with too sure a hold on it. Democracy is not a 'Christian' system, as has been suggested, because it recognises that all men and women are equal and gives them a correspondingly equal share in decision making. But democracy is a system which is in accord with Christian principles, because it reckons that man is fallen; it reckons with original sin. It is the only governmental system which fully caters for man's fallen condition. Democracy is right for us because we are fallen, because none of us can be trusted with power for long, because to put anyone in office in government without virtually telling them that they are on probation, had better watch their step, and can easily be removed next time round, would be to ignore the Fall, to overlook the fact of original sin.

Looking at Ourselves

We have said that this is a book of argument, not of

exhortation, that it is designed to convince, not to convict. Nevertheless, arguments in the theological field, if followed logically, have a nasty habit of turning round to bite the biter. And if we are neither spiritually numb nor morally blind, we know that we do not need to turn to the public scene and the political world to remind ourselves of man's fallen condition. We do not need either to cast our eyes round on our neighbours and acquaintances to register their faults and failings. We only need to look at ourselves and reflect on the immeasurable gap between what we know we ought to do and what we do, the gap between how we ought to think and speak and how we actually think and speak. The reader has only to put this book down for a minute or close the eyes to be able to recall how in the last 24 hours he or she has lived down to the role of the fallen man or woman instead of living up to the role of the redeemed man or woman. He or she needs only to check up his or her recent performance as a child of God against one of those lists of temptations and sins which experienced sinners have devised in order to help us with our self-examination.

As for the writer, it might be salutary for him to put his pen down for a moment and reflect on the gap between his profession and his performance; but it would be sheer self-indulgence to prolong the exercise. For a man must write what he believes to be the truth, whether he manages to live up to it or not. If a minister of the Word had lapsed into inebriety, you would surely not advise him to tear up his Sunday sermon on the Way of Self-Discipline, and instead to exhort his congregation to drown their cares in alcohol. In the upshot there is only one answer for the preacher who wonders whether he is worthy to preach the sermon he has composed or for the writer who wonders whether he is worthy to write the religious book he is working on. The answer is: Of course not. To ask yourself: Am I worthy to perform this Christian task? is really the peak of pride and presumption. For the very question carries the implication that we spend most of our time doing things we are worthy to do. We simply do not have that kind of worth. That is what this chapter is all about, our fallen nature, our corruption by original sin. It is perhaps a topic which an angel would be unfitted by his innocence to talk about.

There is no clear-cut boundary line between public evils and private sins. We have spoken of the social and economic ills that disfigure our world. In turning from them to examine our personal failings we do not cross a frontier. We cannot slide out of all responsibility for what is happening in the wider world by claiming to be powerless and insignificant. We cannot sever ourselves from the community which includes thousands of homeless fellow-creatures. We do not even have the right to detach ourselves in total disgust when we hear that millions of pounds have changed hands between individuals foreseeing and fixing take-over bids. Perhaps we are subtly involved when company mergers seemingly manufacture money out of thin air for the enrichment of everyone financially interested. For public economic injustice is only private selfishness magnified. Corporate covetousness is only private greed aggregated. In any given thought or act today you and I align ourselves either with those who are working out God's purposes here or with those who are rejecting them. So when we fail to restrain our pride, our selfishness, our vanity, or our greed over this or that seemingly trivial matter, we align ourselves with all the world's more ambitious workers of wickedness.

During recent decades there has been a strong emphasis

by many Christian teachers and writers on the relevance of Christianity in the modern world. What has often been urged in the name of this relevance has been the application of Christian moral principles to governmental organisation of social life. We have seen developments such as the National Health Service and the Social Security system as needful practical extensions of the Christian duty to love our neighbours, to care for the disabled, and to visit the fatherless children and the widows in their affliction. These developments are indeed in part the outcome of a specifically Christian appeal to the national conscience made in the earlier decades of our century. 'In place of the conception of the Power-State we are led to that of the Welfare-State' William Temple wrote in *Citizen and Churchman* in 1941. Whether this was the first public use of the expression 'Welfare-State' I do not know, but the *Oxford Dictionary of Quotations* cites it as though indeed it were an epoch-making usage.[2] Yet it has to be said now that there has been no comparable emphasis by Christian teachers and writers on the relevance of Christianity to the modern world in terms of the matters addressed in this book. We have heard less than we should about the application to modern life of basic Christian teaching on the nature of man, his temporal situation here below, and his ultimate destiny.

The Christian thinker has to walk on a tightrope in handling this topic. We all applaud developments in Western societies which have provided safety nets of at least minimal social support for the victims of poverty, disability, and ill-health. At the same time, developments have produced comparative affluence at social levels where people have the wit or the luck to be able to fit themselves neatly into the employment market. It can never be a cause for regret either that people are protected from the extremes of deprivation or that access is increasingly opened to the good things of life. But the surface benefits of civilisation can so easily conceal realities from us. Just as your tinned baked beans and your morning newspaper fail to remind you readily of their ultimate derivation from what grows in the soil and the sun, so your insurance policies and your welfare safeguards tend to chase from the mind your daily dependence on the gifts of health and safety. There is a state of mind on which the sense of life's emergencies never impinges, until one day the unexpected occurs, you are interviewed by the press or the radio reporter, and you confess, 'I never thought it could happen to me'. We have to remind ourselves that it is happening to someone all the time.

The initial argument of this book, then, is that natural afflictions and disasters combine with the effects of human wickedness to produce levels of misery and insecurity on earth from which sensitive men and women cry for deliverance. The cry is for a help beyond what is humanly on offer. As Christians, we are urged to throw ourselves upon God's mercy. Not that mortal life can ever lose its precariousness. Redemption in Christ certainly brings forgiveness, but it brings no automatic cure for deafness or arthritis. Commitment to Christ is not rewarded by comprehensive insurance cover against the ills of mortality. But Christ's role on earth was that of healer as well as forgiver. Moreover, the persistent promise of the Gospel is of everlasting life; and what is everlasting life for if not to fill out the deficiencies and correct the imbalances of life in time? Our Lord's story of Dives and Lazarus (Luke 16:19–31) puts the heaviest possible emphasis on the fact that life after death can reverse the respective roles here below of the comfortable and the deprived.

The issue here, however, is that sensitive men and women, surveying the human scene, will hunger for the kind of spiritual, moral, and indeed intellectual meat which only the Christian faith can supply. Christianity does not speak to the complacent. It is the desperate man or woman whose needs and perplexities are answered, as those of the great converts have been answered. Half-heartedly picking up bits of Christian teaching to decorate a basic fabric of worldly assumptions can satisfy only those who cocoon themselves from reality.

It is when our confidence in earthly things is shaken that the Gospel speaks to us. For the Christian, revelation presents the redeeming work of Christ as a great rescue operation for fallen man. If the liner of worldly self-satisfaction is sinking, comfortable and opulent though it be, it is time to leave it. If the *Titanic* is going down, torn open underneath on the iceberg of human disobedience, then the only hope lies in taking to the boats. It is imprudent at such a crisis to continue to put all our trust in the unsinkable product of advanced modern technology. It is better to be with those who can recognise an emergency when they see one. The Christian knows when to cry, 'Stop the world: I want to get off!' He takes the plunge. Perhaps he can see nothing at all in the darkness of the distant scene, but one step is enough for him, because it is the step that takes him off the edge of the doomed deck. 'Let go hell', as Djuna Barnes put it in *Nightwood*, 'and your fall will be broken by the roof of heaven.'[3] Well, it won't be as quick as all that perhaps. But the boats which keep afloat will bring their passengers by dawn to where a free passage is offered on another vessel and under a different Captain.

The human situation is one of just such emergency. In response, the Christian finds in the Gospel a reality which permeates all life and thought, all culture and enterprise. We cannot get to grips with the emergency if we try to use Christ and his teaching as colourful illustrations in a calendar of personal boosts for the year. It will serve no purpose to turn the pages week by week on a Sunday for visual refreshment before going back to six days of total immersion in the world of getting and spending. We shall misrepresent and abuse the Christian revelation unless we fasten our minds on the issue of salvation — salvation from something so awesomely terrible for the human race that it was worth God's while to see his Son nailed on a cross in the rescue operation.

To any who would suggest that this chapter overstresses the grave condition of humanity, the corruptions of the fallen world, there can be only one reply: What was it, then, that God rescued humanity from at so appalling a cost?

Notes

1 Jonathan Swift, *Gulliver's Travels* (T Nelson and Sons: London, First published 1726), p 140.
2 *The Oxford Dictionary of Quotations*, Third Edition (Oxford University Press: Oxford, 1979), p 532.
3 Djuna Barnes, *Nightwood* (Faber and Faber: London, 1936), p 177.

2
Our Civilisation and the Fall

Nature and the Fall

Many people today voice bewilderment at the condition
of our civilisation. Why is there so much vandalism and
violence, vice and addiction in our cities? The question
is tossed about in the media between politicians and social workers. An angry radical declares that it is all the
product of privation and unemployment. A conservative replies that this is a libel on the unemployed, most
of whom hate violence and vice as much as politicians
do: the trouble stems from lack of respect for authority,
lack of discipline in the schools, lack of parental
firmness at home.... And so on. The blame is shunted
around, this way and that. The philosopher is apt to
think that no simplistic reply to such questions is possible. If Jim has ripped the receiver out of the telephone
kiosk or tripped up an old-age pensioner and snatched
her handbag, no doubt a long list of contributory 'causes'
of the act could be formulated: the boredom of unemployment, the example of violence on television programmes, his parents' former lack of attention to him,
his teachers' failure to engage his interests in worthwhile pursuits, and so on. The list of contributory
'causes' would of course merely share out the blame for
the delinquency, apportioning a little bit here and a little
bit there, but reserving a hefty percentage for Jim's own
sheer ill-will.

The distribution of blame may appear to take in

impersonal causes like 'unemployment' and 'the dereliction of the inner-city environment', but, of course,
these 'causes' are not just given by God, like tornadoes or
earthquakes. They are the product of human decision
making. Various people decided last century to make the
area where Jim now lives a hive of textile-manufactur-
ing. Mills were built to pour out smoke. Railway sidings
were constructed to move the goods. Back-to-back
houses were thrown up in rows to accommodate the
workers as closely as possible to the mills. If you are
going to track down the sinful element in the numerous
decisions that first produced the smoky but flourishing
area of nineteenth-century industry and then converted
it into an area of twentieth-century decay, you will have
to pin-point acts of greed, covetousness, and managerial
tyranny in the lives of dozens of Victorians. Or rather
you will have to disentangle the element of greed and
covetousness in decisions which were perhaps three
parts worthy and disinterested and one part selfish. The
mind boggles at trying to get to the total causal basis of
Jim's act in terms of human carelessness or self-centredness. Plainly, Jim's act is entangled in a network of
human sinfulness. The network is so complex and far-
reaching that even you or I, in buying a cheap imported
blouse or shirt 20 years ago, may have contributed our
little bit to the total pattern of events which destroyed
the textile industry in which Jim might otherwise have
had a satisfying job.

This network of sinfulness is indeed exactly what we
call our 'fallen state'. It knits the nation together. It knits
the human race together. To say that acts of wickedness
are due to defects in the social environment is merely to
shift a proportion of responsibility from malefactors to
others who have acted in the past with intentions which

were either wholly culpable or partly culpable, partly innocent. Thus to attribute the cause of evil to environmental factors of the kind suggested is to spread human culpability very widely indeed. It eventually touches a poor distressed gentlewoman who survives on an old-age pension meagrely supplemented by interest from some stock purchased by her grandfather in a Hong Kong textile firm. She too has a minuscule share in the pattern of causation that produced the dereliction in Jim's home environment.

A Product of the Evolutionary Process

Some theorists have tried to eliminate the responsibility of the human will for wickedness by seeing the antithesis between good and evil as a product of the evolutionary process. It has sometimes been argued that we ought to recognise delinquent behaviour as a survival of forms of action and self-expression which were once necessary and justified but have now outgrown their usefulness. Physical aggression was once necessary, it is argued, in defence of the tribe, and the habit of physical aggression has stuck. Jim's far-off ancestor had to fell and slaughter his opponent to make sure that his family had roast boar for supper, and Jim, by some long-ingrained principle of continuing reflex, assaults the old-age pensioner and rifles her handbag in order to feast on fish and chips. The implication of this reasoning is that Jim is not so much wicked as out of date.

What is interesting about the argument, however, is that it takes the subject of delinquency, of moral evil, and spreads causation through the human race across the map of history. Whether the argument that physical aggression was once necessary or justified and has ingrained itself among reflex human actions can be said to explain anything at all is doubtful. Words can be chosen which, cunningly or carelessly, blur the issue. Expressions such as 'physical aggression' can be evasively used to cover on the one hand, hunting wild animals for food or resisting attack, and on the other hand, assaulting a defenceless innocent, thus blurring the distinction between different moral categories. Nevertheless, the image of aggression spread across the face of history is highly congruous with the Christian picture of a fallen race.

Images of an Unfallen World

There have been those who have tried to picture, by contrast, what an unfallen world would be like. In one of C S Lewis' Narnia stories, a whistle is blown at the end of a meal and immediately responsive mice rush in to eat up all the crumbs from the carpet. This represents a fusion between nature and hygiene, not to say convenience, which would simplify life for us a good deal. Certainly it is of the nature of mice to get rid of crumbs and a world in which they could be trusted to perform this function in the proper place and at the proper time would suit us fine. No more sweeping the floor, no more vacuuming the carpet. And presumably the household cat, if there were one, would restrain its appetite. The thing is conceivable. I once had tea in the garden of a remote country cottage, a café where the cat had got into the habit of jumping up and lapping up spilt milk from the scrubbed wooden tables. Customers were tickled by the practice. They would stroke the cat, then tip milk into saucers for it after they had finished their tea, thus further satisfying it. It was obvious that the proprietors who managed to sell to customers the milk that was to feed their cat could be complimented on their business acumen. But the main point of the story is this: after its other activities, the cat settled down on the ground for a nap, and took no notice at all when a number of field mice ran around within a few inches of its nose. Cat and mice appeared to have reached an accommodation.

The philosopher might suggest that such little events delight us — the mice indoors or the chaffinches and ducks outdoors that clean away our crumbs, and the cat that wipes the milk from the table — because they represent an unfallen state for which we hanker, of which we dream, for which we were intended, and which we have lost.

A world where the activities of mice made vacuum cleaners unnecessary and mousetraps unthinkable would certainly be an ideal one. If it were natural for mice to function as carpet-sweepers and for cats to rest quietly while they got on with the job, then Nature would not be the 'Nature' which Tennyson described as 'red in tooth and claw'.[1] When Milton pictures the Garden of Eden in 'Paradise Lost', he makes it plainly a 'heaven on earth'.[2] There is the whole wealth of Nature in it without any of the inconveniences. We all know full well that for us the difference between Nature in the raw and a garden is a sharp one. Anyone who has taken over a patch of ground from the care of Nature to turn it into a garden knows what a laborious business it can be, not only to tame Nature in the making of the garden, but to keep Nature tamed in the preservation of the garden. Three months' neglect of a garden in a wet English spring or summer will convert it into a wilderness.

Milton takes his cue from the book of Genesis: 'And out of the ground made the Lord God to grow every tree that is pleasant to the sight, and good for food.'³ Pleasant to look at and good to eat. The blend of beauty and usefulness is there from the start, and similarly the blend of the natural and the useful. Milton takes great care to make clear that the rivers watering the garden are at once as beautiful and 'natural' in their meanderings under trees and through the dales as any we have seen, and yet they constitute as efficient an irrigation and drainage system as men could manufacture by constructing a reservoir and laying pipes. Nature presents no problems in the Garden of Eden. We have Nature's profusion without its excess, Nature's beauty without its discomforts, Nature's vitality without its cruelty. For all the beasts of the earth frisk and play around Adam and Eve, even the ones which have since become wild and dangerous. The lion leaps about in fun, dandling a kid in its paws; bears and tigers and leopards gambol around; even the clumsy elephant makes sport of its own clumsiness and magnitude, performing comic party tricks with its trunk before a delighted audience of two.

Adam and Eve themselves stroll hand in hand, Eve's beauty perfectly mirroring the beauty of the natural world around them; her golden hair trailing and waving like a veil about her, its ringlets like the early tendrils of the vine. Adam and Eve stand whispering together in the green shade by a fountain, then sit down and recline on a downy bank sprinkled with flowers. If you have ever tried reclining in the nude on a downy bank sprinkled with flowers, you will know what hidden snares Nature would have in store for you in our fallen world. The softer and mossier the bank, the surer it is that its dampness will seep into your bones and turn you rheumatic. The richer the growth of flowers and grass, the more painfully alive the area will be with creatures that bite the flesh and suck the blood. An hour spent in one of our most beautiful gardens today, behaving as Adam and Eve behaved, and our skin would be a mass of itching lumps. But, of course, Milton knew well what he was doing when he pictured his heaven on earth. He was purposely conjuring up the sheer overflowing plentifulness of natural vegetation without its concomitant disadvantages. The word 'garden' itself connotes an area of natural growth which is controlled and ordered. Milton uses at one and the same time words which recall the abundant richness of the natural scene and words which suggest the deliberately ordered neatness of a country estate.

An outer world where Nature behaves is as idealistic a conception as a human world where natural instincts and appetites are fully controlled. Such harmony does not obtain in the fallen world. Indeed, the fact of the Fall means that Christian teaching must be much concerned with moral conflict and have recourse to battle imagery in defining the human situation. There is the struggle between flesh and spirit, between nature and grace, between what we want to do and what we ought to do. What seems natural to us is not necessarily right for us. In this respect there is a clear correspondence between, say, pruning fruit trees and extirpating weeds on the one hand, and controlling our own natural inclinations and appetites on the other hand.

The example of pruning fruit trees is a very gentle instance of what grappling with the excesses of Nature can mean. People who live in the British Isles do not have to live in conditions which are a continual reminder of the hostile power of Nature in its more brutal and painful aspects. A stroll off the road in the countryside is not likely to bring an encounter with a poisonous snake or a hungry lion. There is nothing of the fearsome insect and animal life of the African jungle. It is safe to turn the car off the main road to explore some quiet side-road, for there will be no danger even if two tyres burst and the petrol runs out. But to explore thus in the Arizona desert and to run out of petrol might be fatal. There is neither murderously scorching heat nor murderously freezing cold to deal with in the British Isles. There are neither tornadoes nor earthquakes. It is all the easier for the inhabitants to lose all sense of how sharp is the contrast between Nature in the raw and Nature tamed.

When I paid my first visit to the United States of America in the 1960s, it was still possible to travel conveniently about the country by railway, and it was such travel that left me with my vividest memory of the country. I had travelled across the Atlantic in the *Queen Mary* in early March. The voyage was unusually rough. For a couple of days the hatches were battened down, passengers were kept below, the floors and stairs rocked and swayed under our feet. Yet not for a moment did I have any acute sense of the menacing power of Nature to damage and destroy. It was to be left to a train journey to produce such a sense. I took a night train from Detroit to St Louis. Almost everything on that journey has long faded from my memory, but one thing sticks vividly in my mind — the memory of eating breakfast next morning and staring out of the carriage window as the train crossed the Mississippi.

An Englishman's idea of a river is one thing and an American's idea is another thing. I found the sheer magnitude of the Mississippi overwhelming, that enormous expanse of rolling brown water, so vast, so disturbingly close beneath the carriage window. The crawling train, snaking its way across the bridge seemingly a few feet

above this heaving mass of mud-stained water, appeared
to be a terrifyingly frail thing by comparison. The word
'river' acquired a new connotation. It could no longer be
associated simply with the Swale or the Wharfe, or even
the Tay or the Thames. The experience brought to life
one of the most impressive passages in the poetry of T S
Eliot. Born and reared in St Louis, Eliot has left us an un-
nerving picture of the Mississippi with all its menacing
power in *Four Quartets*.

> I do not know much about gods; but I think
>   that the river
> Is a strong brown god — sullen, untamed and
>   intractable,
> Patient to some degree, at first recognised as a
>   frontier;
> Useful, untrustworthy, as a conveyor of
>   commerce;
> Then only a problem confronting the builder
>   of bridges.
> The problem once solved, the brown god is
>   almost forgotten
> By the dwellers in cities — ever, however,
>   implacable,
> Keeping his seasons and rages, destroyer,
>   reminder
> Of what men choose to forget.[4]

Before pressing the full significance of Eliot's sense of
the sullen, untameable power of the 'strong brown god',
let us reflect on another aspect of Nature's power which
the inhabitant of the British Isles is likely to be less sensitive to than an inhabitant of a continent where Nature's
power impends over people with a more awesome

immensity. On a visit to the United States in the 1970s, I was once more overwhelmed by an impression of Nature's power which this time came from travel by air. Flying from New York to Nashville, Tennessee, and happening to catch glimpses of the terrain beneath us, I was astonished at the enormous extent of the forestation. Mile after mile, up hill and down dale, forested areas spread with a magnitude which made the mind boggle. How absurdly thin, petty, and frail was that network of tiny roads. How tentative, after all, was man's grip on these immeasurable areas of natural growth.

The United States has one of the most advanced, highly technologised civilisations in human history, yet here was a European visitor pre-eminently struck by the tenuousness of civilised man's grip on the forces of Nature. Frail and precarious seemed the railway bridge over the untameable Mississippi. Frail and precarious seemed the network of roads threading their way through the encroaching forests.

The Basis of Civilisation

Man's civilisation has been built by the conquest and taming of Nature. We have domesticated the earth by constructing material frameworks and networks for our protection and convenience. The 'frameworks' are the houses that shelter us from the elements, the villages and cities in which we have established communal life. The 'networks' are those systems of connecting pipes and wires for water, gas, sewage disposal, electrical power and telephone, which free us from the need to battle more directly against Nature day by day by chopping up wood to keep ourselves warm, carrying water from streams to quench our thirst, and digging the soil to bury our waste. The 'networks' are also those linkages provided by roads and bridges, by railways and tunnels, by airports and runways. This taming of the jungle has increased our freedom. We do not have to spend time fetching water from a spring when we want to wash our hands. Civilisation, by imposing a vast material framework and a vast material network on the natural order, has given us the freedom to travel, to study, to develop arts and sciences. And in spite of all the tangle of regulations we have to submit to when we want to make use of roads, airports, gas taps, and electric points, we do not consider that our freedom is thereby in any degree impaired. We do not jib at traffic control as an inhibition or at regulations about the appropriate ampage of fuse-wire for this or that appliance as a grave restriction of our liberties.

This point is made because our civilisation in its moral and cultural as well as in its material aspects has been built by the imposition of frameworks and networks to conquer and tame natural impulses and thereby grant us a freedom we should otherwise lack. Is not the framework of law, within which we live socially, comparable to the material framework of house and village and city? Is not the network of legislation, and of judicial machinery and procedure which safeguards us socially and morally comparable to the network of roads and pipes and wires which safeguard us physically and give us freedom to attend to matters other than the immediate search for life's physical necessities?

There is nothing remarkable about this comparison. The social and moral upbringing of the young in the family mirrors the process of taming Nature which we have seen in the wider field of public progress from jungle to city. This is plain whether you are teaching a child to walk, to eat decently, or to make hygienic use of a toilet. Indeed, in the poem quoted above, T S Eliot goes on to make the comparison specifically. First, he observes that we are too ready to forget the menacing power of un-tamed Nature. We build a bridge and then think no more about it until one day it is swept away in a flood. The appalling power of the 'strong brown god', its potential even after seeming tamed at any moment to rage and de-stroy, is something we ought not to forget. Then he adds, 'The river is within us'. There is the same natural force within us which must be tamed as Nature has been tamed in the outer world. And the taming of natural forces within us is just as much a matter of imposing frame-works and networks as is the taming of natural forces outside us. Nurturing the young morally and socially means introducing them to a framework of moral prin ci-ples and a network of restraints, inhibitions, and cour-tesies which ease social communication as the road or the telephone eases physical communication.

The process of education shows the same principles operative in the intellectual field as are operative mor-ally and socially in the upbringing of children at home, and again the process by which man has tamed external Nature is mirrored. For traditionally the teacher's task has been assumed to be that of introducing the pupil to a cultural inheritance in the way of arts and sciences, each of which has its own framework of substance and princi-ple, its own network of rule and regulation. You cannot solve an equation, sculpt a statue, locate a star, translate a poem, or diagnose a disease except by accommodating yourself submissively to a systematised body of know-ledge and expertise, a framework of theoretical and prac-tical fact, and a network of regulations for deduction or procedure.

There is today a body of thinking which tends to derive all value and meaning from nature in the raw. For secularised popular philosophy has bred a notion of progress and development which takes its pattern from the way natural things grow or gush — a flower, a tree, a river, an oil-well — and not from the way Nature has been tamed and civilisation built. This is the root from which fashionable notions of self-cultivation and self-expression derive. We shall have to turn later to the Alternative Ethic which has corrupted even 'Christian' teachers in this respect. Our civilisation in its material aspects has been built by the imposition upon the natural order of the frameworks and networks which give us homes and cities, water-taps and telephones. Our civilisation in its moral, social, and cultural aspects has been built by the imposition upon natural forces of frameworks and networks which give us the family, the state, the nation, our system of justice, our culture, with its codes, its etiquettes, and its artistic achievements.

Yet now, after centuries of civilising by restraint and regulation in relation to principle and code, we suddenly find about us influential mentors who believe and teach that individual and social progress depend, not on accommodating human beings to the great frameworks of established justice, order, and culture, but in asserting the self rebelliously against every form or formulation, every principle or rule, on the assumption that value and meaning derive from something which springs up spontaneously within the untutored, undisciplined ego. This is the anarchic philosophy which possesses ('possesses' is the word) the minds of many who mould the thinking of future generations in the school classroom, in the television studio, sometimes, alas, even in the church.

There is one thing on which Christians see eye to eye with those pioneers in the past who have pushed back the frontiers of barbarism and given us our civilisation. It is that progress depends on conquering the natural, on taming the 'strong brown god', whether it is the flooding river outside us or the flow of appetite and passion within us. It is, historically speaking, both a very old — and a very new — idea, that instead of channelling and bridging, reining and overpowering, the energies of the 'strong brown god', we should fall down and worship him. Indeed, it is a pre-civilisational notion. It is also, alas, a post-civilisational notion.

The Christian, in accepting the reality of the supernatural, allows to the natural the status of that which has to be restrained, disciplined, and controlled. In doing so, he is of course on the side of civilisation and culture. The contemporary secularist, in so far as he subscribes to the fashionable code of rejecting disciplines and restraints in the interests of supposed unfettered self-expression, is on the side of barbarism. He is preaching a return to the jungle. And he is getting it — through addiction to the bottle and the needle. It is painfully ironic that the great exponents of self-cultivation and self-expression so often end up in abject servitude to drugs that numb the mind and destroy the body. This is Nature's revenge, living evidence that you will either tame her or be tamed by her. The 'strong brown god' remains implacable. Ultimately, only the power of the Holy Spirit can deal with him. He is one of those 'rulers of the darkness of this world' against whom St Paul warns us to take up 'the sword of the Spirit' (Eph 6:12 and 17). He is to be resisted, or he will enslave.

Milton realised this. Once his Eve has eaten of the forbidden fruit she turns to the tree in adoration:

> O Sovereign, virtuous, precious of all Trees
> In Paradise.[5]

The first lines of praise hint at the enormity of what she has done. For her words glorifying the 'precious Tree', the fruit that hangs on it 'offered free to all', sound ironically parodic echoes of hymns to the Cross and to the Fruit of the Virgin's womb who hung upon it, 'offered free to all'. This ghastly parody of Christian worship here addressed to the growth of Nature is directly in line with the philosophical positions adopted today in our own century, some of them nourished by otherwise well-meaning thinkers and writers. So Eve, leaving the tree to return to Adam, first genuflects before it, doing the kind of reverence with which one might leave a royal presence.

It might be argued that since 'Nature' as previously described in Milton's Garden of Eden is free of excess, cruelty and poison, Eve's reverence before the tree is less culpable than the reverence of twentieth-century idolators of the natural. Milton of course makes quite clear that from the first plucking and eating of the apple Nature herself is affected.

> So saying, her rash hand in evil hour
> Forth reaching to the Fruits she plucked, she ate;
> Earth felt the wound.[6]

Nature is wounded, damaged. And the wounds here received by Nature will have to be paid for by wounds endured upon another tree.

There are wounds which are fatal and there are wounds which can be healed. There are sicknesses which are fatal and there are sicknesses which can be cured. The fallen state of humanity is a sickness for which there *is* a remedy. But a grave sickness is unlikely to be cured unless the victims face up to the realities of their condition. That does not mean that they must be always talking about their condition. Indeed, we admire those who, whether their physical problem is temporary or permanent, refuse to sentimentalise or dramatise their disabilities. I met an old friend last week who has Parkinson's disease. 'I've got my pills,' he said, 'but the doctors don't know whether I shall ever fully recover.' He was plainly anxious neither to whine about his illness nor to pretend that it did not exist. I also exchanged a few words with a lady who has multiple sclerosis and rides about on a motorised invalid vehicle rather like a golfing buggy. I admired the vehicle. 'Yes,' she replied, 'but it's really a very extravagant way of taking the dog for a walk!'

We must not pretend that for a disabled person to focus on other things than his or her condition when talking to others is the same thing as ignoring that condition. The disabled or diseased person can look you cheerfully in the eye without a breath of reference to their condition only because in practical matters they have concentrated on coping with that condition. The young lady who has a kidney disease can behave for most of the time as if she has not got the disease only because she spends half an hour three times each day linked up to a dialysis machine.

It is plain that if Christians tried to go through life with little on their minds or their lips except the perilous condition of fallen humanity, they would scarcely fulfil the Gospel call to rejoice and be exceeding glad. They are specifically enjoined to remember with joy that their reward in heaven will be great. Yet to reflect and behave from hour to hour as though the human race were in a state of spiritual and moral health would be culpably absurd. A balance has to be struck. If what a fellow human being needs most at a given time is a hot meal and a bed for the night, reminders of mankind's sinful fallen condition are likely to be out of place. Indeed, they are also likely to be superfluous. Try to impress upon a hungry, jobless, houseless fellow that the human race is given over to pride and self-centredness, and he may well reply, 'You're telling me, mate'. Indeed, he knows in his bones, better than you or I, that the world is not what it ought to be. But the great Christian teachers have always insisted that we shall bring the needed practical and spiritual aid to others effectively only if we ourselves have faced up to our own condition and tried to deal with it. Like the girl with the kidney disease, we shall have zest and cheerfulness for the daily task only if we have spent our daily three half-hours linked up for the spiritual dialysis which filters out of our system what would otherwise clog its channels of vitality and destroy it.

Christianity and Secularism

We live in a society in which, by and large, the fact of the Fall has been ignored and forgotten. That is the condition of the post-Christian West. It is the essence of what we call modern secularism that the fallen condition of humanity is ignored. Thus diagnoses of the human predicament are devised, and prescriptions for human betterment are proposed which ignore the central cause of all malaise, criminality, and disorder. In short, the ultimate result of the Fall of man is ignorance of the Fall.

And since the fallen condition of humanity is ignored, it is scarcely surprising that the offer of salvation is ignored too. Christians tax themselves tirelessly with the questions: Why is the Gospel of Christ not listened to? Why does the offer of redemption not 'speak' as it once spoke to the minds and hearts of our fellow-citizens? It is like asking why men and women who are confident in their health and vigour do not rush off to hospitals for emergency operations. The Church is offering intensive care with a link-up to the drip-feed from the saving blood to men and women who are very well, thank you. Even if they are not feeling very well, thank you, and indeed are deeply unhappy and dissatisfied, they have been instructed from their childhood by every device of education and every influence of the media, that their condition is not a spiritual sickness but a psycho-physical inadequacy which anodynes and boosters can effectively repair or alleviate.

To describe the state of mind of modern secularism as one that ignores the Fall and therefore can feel no need for redemption is not necessarily to provoke challenge or disagreement. Many an atheist and many an agnostic would agree with us. The modern mind does ignore the Fall because it does not believe in the Fall. One might think that confusion could scarcely arise in dispute where positions are as clear as that. Unfortunately, the infection of modern secularist thinking has so permeated the minds of well-meaning Christians that they too become forgetful of man's fallen condition. And to become neglectful of man's fallen condition is, as we shall see later, to knock the meat out of the doctrine of redemption, to empty it of its relevance to a living human emergency; in short, to turn the doctrine of the saving blood into an expensive unit for the provision of kidney dialysis in a country where kidney disease is unknown. The wonderful machine can be admired for the imagination manifested in its devising and the skill displayed in its construction. But it is nothing more than a white elephant in a land where all kidneys work beautifully.

A word of caution is due here about the use of expressions such as 'secular civilisation', 'secular thinking', and 'secular humanism'. Some Christian writers tend to use the word 'secular' as a disapproval noise, and that is a most improper verbal habit. It is a different matter to give a pejorative flavour to our use of the word 'secularism', for in fact the connotational gap between the two words 'secular' and 'secularism' is a wide one; and we do not generally have to make a connotational leap when moving from a descriptive adjective like 'secular' to its corresponding abstract noun. Consider the close relationship between 'Christian' and 'Christianity' or between 'vegetarian' and 'vegetarianism'. The relationship between 'secular' and 'secularism' is not comparable: it is more like the uncomfortable relationship between the neutral word 'race' and the loaded word 'racism'.

The *Oxford English Dictionary* defines 'secular' as 'of or pertaining to the world'.[7] There is no pejorative flavour there. Indeed, the word was once applied regularly to clergy running parishes as opposed to clergy living in religious communities, the secular clergy as opposed to the religious clergy. In such usage the word 'secular' has no pejorative overtones. It opposes this-worldly concerns to other-worldly concerns. The 'secular' is contrasted with the 'religious' in the sense that digging a garden is one thing and praying is another thing. The Christian's duty may well be to dig and pray with equal regularity.

By contrast, the *Oxford English Dictionary* definition

of 'secularism' is 'the doctrine that morality should be based solely on regard to the well-being of mankind in the present life, to the exclusion of all considerations drawn from belief in God or in a future state'.[8] 'Secularist' is defined as 'an adherent of secularism'.[9] So while 'secular' is a purely neutral term, 'secularism' represents a view of life which challenges Christianity head on, for it excludes all considerations drawn from a belief in God or in a future state.

The secular sphere in itself presents no challenge to Christianity. It is the sphere of activity in which most Christians operate for most of their lives. Printing a book is a secular activity whether the book in question is a comic novel or the Bible. The Bible itself, as a material object, as printed pages bound together in a volume, is a product of secular labour. Our Lord was a carpenter, and carpentry is in itself a secular activity whether the artifact manufactured be a dining-room table or a pulpit. The one, of course, is put to a secular use, the other to a religious use. Engaging in secular activities plainly does not make anyone a 'secularist', an exponent or adherent of 'secularism'. In the same way, eating a meal of cheese and salad will not make you a vegetarian. Indeed, living on eggs and cheese and salad for a year will not make you a vegetarian, unless you hold and profess the view that the exclusion of meat from diet is a matter of principle. Vegetarianism excludes meat-eating as a matter of principle, and secularism excludes consideration of God and the religious dimension as a matter of principle.

Thus the distinction between Christianity and secularism is such that the two must always collide, but the distinction between the religious and the secular is like the distinction between the right hand and the left. Involvement in secular activities no more commits you to secularism than involvement, say, in human activities commits you to humanism. Our linguistic usages are odd in this respect. You only need to commit one murder to be a murderer, but a dozen meals of vegetables will not necessarily turn you into a vegetarian. You only need to tell one lie to become a liar, but telling the truth for a whole day will not necessarily turn you into an honest man.

This is an attempt to clear the verbal atmosphere, in particular to put the word 'secularism' in the company in which it belongs. It defines a kind of faith, a restrictive, indeed a negative faith, as we shall see if we put it alongside words which work comparably. The ordinary meat-eater cannot be accused of inconsistency if he is caught one day eating a salad, but the 'vegetarian' loses the right to the label if he is caught one day eating a steak. Drinking a glass of Coke will not make a man a teetotaller, but drinking a single glass of beer will finish a man off as a teetotaller. Saying one prayer may not make you a Christian, but it will finish you off as a bona fide secularist. That is the crucial point. The Christian indulges in secular activities year after year without thus compromising his commitment to Christianity. But a man cannot say a single prayer without compromising his commitment to secularism. In short, like 'teetotalism' and 'vegetarianism', 'secularism' is a noun whose connotation involves a crucial exclusion.

The secularist's position can be defined only in negatives. There is no life except this life in time. There is no order of being except this which we explore with our senses and our instruments. There is no condition of well-being except that of healthy and comfortable life in time. There is no God to be worshipped, for no God created us. There is no God to propitiate, for there is no

God to offend. There is no reward to be sought and no punishment to be avoided except those which derive from earthly authority. There is no law to be obeyed except those which earthly authority imposes or earthly prudence recommends.

No Christian thinks it possible to live without secular activities. No Christian wants to abolish building houses or eating meals. But secularism, by definition, excludes Christian faith and practice. No Christian is trying to prohibit ploughing fields or selling potatoes on the grounds that these are secular activities, but secularists are committed to reject every activity that is religious. Christianity wants to *claim* the secular sphere; secularism wants to *abolish* the religious sphere. So who are the excluders, the narrow prohibitionists? We Christians who do not dispute the value of secular activities and secular motives, but who say, 'We must have something else as well'? Or secularists who deny the validity of religious activity and motivation? Who are the excluders, the bearers of fetters, the shutters-off of avenues, the closers of minds?

We have allowed too much woolly thinking on this issue. Exponents of secularism talk as though Christian teaching closes off options, while their teaching opens doors. The very reverse is true. They talk as though Christianity is restrictive while secularism is open-minded. It is nonsense. Secularism by definition is so closed-minded that it is trying to shut off from the minds of contemporary men and women, boys and girls, the faith, the hope, and the vision that stabilised and enriched the lives of the generations who built our civilisation and gave us our culture. Secularism is an attempt to fetter, to limit, to prohibit. It is a new form of slavery.

Secularism enslaves because a limited secular motivation towards keeping fit, making money, living comfortably, enjoying food, sex, entertainment, travel, family life, and sociability consists in pursuing a sense of well-being appropriate for intelligent animals but not for God's children. Needless to say, even such limited well-being is becoming more and more obviously elusive as the old religious sanctions which disciplined its pursuit are forgotten or scrapped. As the human failures to achieve a tolerable sense of animal well-being become self-evidently more and more numerous, recourse is had to roundabout recipes for boosting self-confidence, for sharpening the responsiveness of the human antennae to what brings earthly satisfaction and pleasure, or for numbing the inner disquiet of the spirit. The Christian knows that no amount of aesthetic stimulus for the emotions or psychiatry for the mind can touch the heart of the human problem. For the human problem is the Fall. Men and women are creatures of a different order from the order in which iniquity and dissension, failure and frustration, injustice and privation, by the very nature of things often prevail. Men and women have dimensions of being which secular earthly aspiration and motivation can never properly cater for. Men and women by creation and vocation are designed and destined for something other than this. In short, they are fallen from what properly appertains to them. They simply are not and never can be fully at home in a sphere of being where aspirations are negated and good purposes fail in their objectives. This is their discomfort: that they demand satisfaction and fulfilments which earthly life can never supply; that they yearn for permanences of love and vitality which a temporal span can never allow for. A quarter of the world's poetry is an anguished, or at least a restless cry from the human heart that what life provides in a world where beauty fades and love dies is not enough.

The reader will observe, as our argument is developed, that the only truly worthwhile aspect of the human being's situation is that he is fallen. For that is the root of his unease in his present home. And his unease is his chief glory. The unease means that, though he may relish and appreciate good food and drink, he cannot come to terms with a world where the subtlest and most refined pleasures of the palate are cherished and indulged in one corner of it while children and adults starve to death through lack of a crust or a drink of water in another corner. Human beings cannot reconcile themselves to such injustices. And if it is argued that such injustices could be removed by the proper exercise of human good will and ingenuity, then the reply must be that it is precisely such good will and ingenuity that are lacking on a sufficient scale to be exercised in solving the problem. The good will and ingenuity are lacking because man is a fallen being. The argument comes full circle.

A civilisation which has secularised all its thinking presupposes that man has no supernatural affiliation. It assumes that, in so far as things go wrong with him, in so far as he falls short of achieving what is desirable and worthwhile, that is not a matter of failure in obligation or obedience to supernatural authority. Its government, its forward planning, its educational system for the most part proceed on the assumption that what is wrong human purpose and ingenuity can put right. We write, 'for the most part' because there are obviously, here and there in the system, individual Christians working with other ends and other priorities at the back of their minds even though they may not always be able to bring them to bear directly and effectively on their professional activities. Such cases notwithstanding, a civilisation which has robbed its intents and ideals of supernatural orientation and has desacralised not only its public thought-life, but also to a large extent its private love life and family life, must inevitably lose all sense of man's fallen condition. For it loses all awareness of transcendent standards and values in relation to which human purpose and endeavour fall short. Therefore it persists in making prescriptions for ameliorating human life and human welfare on the basis of a closed human universe whose inhabitants need no external aid.

There has been plenty of evidence in the history of our century that unaided man is incapable of governing himself or even, it now seems, in sheer self-interest of looking after the earth he inhabits and on which he feeds. Yet we continue to be astonished at the failure of human projects and the degeneration of human beings, and search obdurately for causes and remedies where they can never be found. Tower blocks housing thousands of citizens turn out to have been shoddily built and have to be dynamited to the ground. ('There must be more efficient management and oversight of the work-force in future.') Addiction claims thousands of young healthy bodies for lives of sickness and agony. Homosexuality and promiscuity threaten thousands with an incurably debilitating disease. And the wise legislators of the age solemnly declare, 'The public must be educated against addiction, against AIDS, against alcoholism.' Education is the answer to all our problems.

Education, however, if it is divested of all religious base and sanction, will merely intensify and prolong man's blinkered confinement to this-worldly ends and

aims which have so signally failed us in the past. The
nurturing of the individual's personality and talents is
always laudable. But if the nurturing proceeds wholly
within the mental framework of ideals and practices
which never reach out of time, it can never produce an
understanding of the real nature of the human situation
or the character of human need. It would be over-
simplistic to say that education stands in relation to
humanism as regeneration stands in relation to Christianity, for education can be undertaken and imbued by
purposes rooted in Christian faith, but education bereft
of any awareness of the Christian doctrine of man and
centred wholly in this-worldly criteria partakes of the
nature of everything that is fully secularised. In its
spiritually fettering influence on those who are essentially children of God, its function is to reduce to
materialistic servitude. Education is a nurturing of
human beings in humanity. The ultimate purpose of
humanity is the service of God. Therefore totally secularised education is a contradiction in terms.

We have already made clear that no intelligent Christian will idealise the past. Nevertheless, we cannot but be
aware that the orthodox view of man's situation and his
destiny once had an authority in public affairs, such as
education, which it has now lost. Christians have tended
to respond to this situation by preserving their own
spiritual commitment and duties of public worship, and
jogging along as best they can at the side of unbelievers,
even when they and their colleagues are commonly en-
gaged in the moulding of minds and attitudes in education, journalism, or politics. And yet there can surely be
no honest compromise of final motivation between
those who believe that the finite system we inhabit from
the cradle to the grave is the total sum of things and those

who hold that we are pilgrims of eternity making a brief journey through time, and that everything in this life that deeply matters points elsewhere. For the secularist, death is the end and this world is opaque. For the Christian, death is the beginning and this world is open to the eternal.

Here is no intention to depreciate the value of our secular civilisation and its culture. On the contrary, Christianity, we have said, wants to claim the secular, to subsume it, for it is that sphere of things which ought to be enjoyed and used to the ultimate end of serving God. Yet today especially, when we ponder into whose hands we have increasingly consigned the keeping of our cultural inheritance and the responsibility of transmitting it to later generations, can we feel other than deeply worried? And can we avoid the additional sense of guilt in that so much that we have inherited in our educational system, our art, our buildings, and our literature was bequeathed to us by God-fearing men and women who at least *tried* to set their hearts on things above?

In education and the media, for instance, we have today at our disposal the most potent mind-moulding apparatus ever devised. Can we pretend that this apparatus is in the right hands? Can we pretend that it is used, by and large, for the service of God and the nourishment of his children in that service? Can we pretend that it is used, by and large, to recommend the life of virtue and self-discipline? Consider what eccentric and amoral 'ideals' of human self-expression are widely canvassed among our intelligentsia; then ask ourself what is being urged upon the young today in our educational institutions as a pattern of the good life and a recipe for happiness. And what models of satisfaction and self-fulfilment are set before us as we assimilate what is presented to us by the media and the advertisers?

Our over-riding public problem today is that the control of the secular sphere is increasingly in the hands of secularists. And the secular sphere is far too precious, far too important, to be left in the hands of secularists. Secularists are the last people to be entrusted with control of things secular. It is like putting the control of the world's money into the hands of misers. It is like putting pederasts in charge of a nursery. For the secular is that sphere of things which ought to be used by God's children in the service and love of God and each other. The secular is that sphere of things which ought to be used and enjoyed to the ultimate end of serving God and man. Secularists believe that the secular is to be experienced and enjoyed for its own sake, as misers believe that money is to be accumulated and gloated over for its own sake. The more we examine our current situation, the more we realise that this is no time for Christians to neglect, depreciate, or shun the secular world. For the secular world must be rescued from secularists. That is a most pressing Christian vocation today, to wrest the control of the secular sphere from the grip of secularists.

Notes

1 Alfred Tennyson, 'In Memoriam AHH', *Poems and Plays* (Oxford University Press: London, 1968), p 243.

2 John Milton, 'Paradise Lost', *The Poetical Works of Milton* (A Donaldson: Edinburgh, 1772).

3 Milton, *ibid*.

4 T S Eliot, 'The Dry Salvages', *Four Quartets* (Faber and Faber: London, 1944), p 25. Quoted by kind permission of Faber and Faber.

5 Milton, *op cit.*
6 Milton, *ibid.*
7 *The Oxford English Dictionary* (Oxford University Press: Oxford, 1984).
8 *The Oxford English Dictionary, ibid.*
9 *The Oxford English Dictionary, ibid.*

3
Redemption in Christ

The Gift of Redemption

It might be argued that enough has now been said about the fallen state of mankind, that Christianity is a religion of joy and hope, of redemption and salvation. When I turn to *The Oxford Dictionary of the Christian Church*, I find 'redemption' thus defined: 'It is viewed by theologians under the double aspect of deliverance from sin and restoration of man and the world to communion with God'.[1] 'Deliverance' and 'restoration': the words carry the mind back to a situation from which deliverance is required and restoration sought. When we talk to people who are acutely conscious of the gift of salvation in Christ, we find that there is a limit to what they can say of the joy of being redeemed. A few words, 'peace', 'happiness', 'delight', and 'gratitude' will exhaust the vocabulary of human joy in salvation. Indeed, it has been justly observed that even the greatest poets cannot sustain for long the verbal record of bliss.

Perhaps only in music can a mood of sheer unbroken, unclouded happiness be long sustained. A Beethoven symphony — the fifth, the sixth, or the seventh — may end in a last movement which constitutes a full-length expression of joy and exhilaration. After the moods of tension, brooding, and conflict seemingly voiced in earlier movements of the symphony, the resolution of greyness or darkness into light can be fully voiced in a final movement which not only makes its point, but hammers it home repeatedly, exultantly. But the novelist, say, could scarcely emulate such an achievement. When we have lived through all Jane Eyre's agonies and struggles, her tortuous wrestlings between heart and conscience, we have to be satisfied in the final resolution with four words: 'Reader, I married him!'[2]

If you have been in the company of Christians deeply conscious of their happiness in the knowledge of Christ's saving love, you will find that when they talk about it, their minds tend to go back to their former pre-conversion days and to the experience of conversion itself. One man recalls walking at a particular point in a particular street on a certain day when the divine hand seemed suddenly to descend and close around him. Another recalls the opening of a door which not only let him into a new acquaintance's house, but also into a divine presence which he has never since parted company with. St Augustine recalls going into the garden of his lodgings one day with his friend Alypius, and another day, alone with his mother, leaning out of a window looking over the garden of a house in Ostia. C S Lewis speaks of a ride between Magdalen College and Headington on a number 2 bus and of a trip to Whipsnade Zoo. In such images are contained the recollections of great transitions across canyons separating worry from joy, doubt from faith. But, as Jane Eyre summed up the future life of joy and fulfilment in the four words, 'Reader, I married him', the autobiographical record of conversion tends to conclude, 'Reader, I found Him'.

That is how we are made. Our joys are measured by the miseries we have escaped from. We cannot expatiate at great length about the health we currently enjoy, but we can be eloquent about the illnesses from which we have recovered. An old friend of mine, an American, who died after a heroic struggle with cancer, and who had such sturdy Christian faith that he could exercise his acute sense of humour at the expense of his own condition, once told me, 'When I go to a dinner party, I make a bargain. I say, "I won't talk about my operations if you won't show me your slides".' When a few years ago I suffered from a slipped disc, I found that the subject had only to be mentioned to bring me into communion with one-time fellow-sufferers. J B Priestley once said that he had no time for a man who could not sustain half-an-hour's conversation on the varieties of pipe-tobacco. I found I had entered via a slipped disc into a world-wide fellowship in which the password 'back trouble' would key off reminiscences of extraordinary variety and length. The local garage proprietor, the man who called with the fish-van, the retired consultant in the next village, even my American publisher when I met him face to face could look back on past dorsal agonies and recount in detail the moment and mode of relief that ended them. 'I crawled up the stairs to the physiotherapist's room on my hands and knees. Half an hour later I strode down the same staircase and galloped back to my car.' This was the sudden conversion story, St Paul on the road to Damascus. There were other more gradual conversions from illness to health, the fruit of much patient supinity on hard floors and therapeutic beds. But the joy of health lay in the knowledge of illness conquered.

We should not be surprised when autobiographical records of conversion turn out to dwell more on past sins than on present relief from sin. It smacks of smugness to dilate on present joy and good fortune. In any case, the very nature of Christian relief in trusting to the saving blood of Christ is such that talk of the self's blessedness would be out of place. Men and women can talk at length about their past sins because after all they were their own sins; they themselves committed them. But to talk about salvation is to talk about something freely given, something to which the self has made no contribution except in the limited sense of asking for it as something desperately needed. Our sins are our own, spiritually speaking our only self-chosen possessions, the only things which utterly and exclusively belong to us. We have scarcely the right to speak by contrast of 'our salvation' because in the strictest sense it is not ours. Salvation is what Christ's redemptive act offers to the world. The very desperation of the human condition as explored in past chapters of this book, the seeming hopelessness of our entanglement in the network of human disobedience, the seeming absurdity of imagining that at the public level there could ever be sweetness and light, peace and harmony, in place of meanness and injustice, violence and greed — all this plain evidence of our fallen condition is also evidence that of our own accord we cannot rise again.

It is not remarkable then that saintly souls who have felt the full blessings of God's forgiveness should dwell rather on God's goodness than on their own happiness. Indeed, the happiness itself consists in an escape from the level of being at which my having this or not having that is a prevailing theme. Today is a beautiful day of early September. I look out of my study window to see the flanks of Skiddaw on the other side of the valley coated with purple heather. The sky is blue, the white clouds are few and far between, the sun shines down. It is beautiful. That is the right initial reponse. Surely not, in the first place, 'How blessed am I to be able to survey such a scene!' That might sound too much like gloating.

I could scarcely say it or even think it without recalling how many holiday-makers throughout the month of August lived through days of wind and rain, cloud and storm in the hope of some such never-to-be-tasted hours of clement tranquillity. On the other hand, would it not be churlish to fail to add to gratitude for the scene before me, gratitude for the fact that I have eyesight to enjoy it, physical mobility to explore it, and freedom from any disability that might mar my relish of the world?

Here one has to tread carefully. Am I not in danger of congratulating myself on possessing what my blind neighbour lacks, what my crippled neighbour lacks? Am I congratulating myself because it is Mrs X and not I who has multiple sclerosis, and Mr Y and not I who has Parkinson's disease? There is surely danger whenever we turn from admiring contemplation of the other to satisfied or even grateful contemplation of the self. The hills and the trees, the blue sky and the white clouds have been given to us. That fact requires us to turn our hearts elsewhere in gratitude. Our eyesight, our hearing, and our mobility have been given to us. That fact requires us to turn our hearts elsewhere in gratitude. The difference between ingratitude and gratitude is not the difference between grumbling about what we lack and congratulating ourselves on what we have got. It is not the difference between saying, 'How unfortunate, or ill-used, I am' and saying, 'How lucky and favoured I am'. It is the difference between thinking about ourselves, whether miserably or smugly, and thinking about someone else, in this case God the Giver in recognition of our unworthiness.

Suspect the voice that only wants to proclaim aloud the blessed happiness of being saved in Jesus Christ. For the eyes and the heart that are truly turned on our Lord will not be overcome solely with delight in what they now enjoy. They will be conscious of their own unworthiness. Those who truly love him will talk of his goodness more than of their own blessedness, of his mercy more than of their forgiveness, of what he gives more than of what they receive. If the convert, like St Augustine, seems to dwell overmuch on his own wickedness and folly in pre-conversion days, is not this the reverse side of the coin of worship? Does it not imply enormous gratitude for the mercy that has lifted such a load? Awareness of the burdensome weight that has been removed lingers with the forgiven sinner as details of past ailments linger in the mind of the man restored to health. What we cannot avoid noticing, if we read carefully records such as St Augustine's, is that when his eyes are turned upon himself, it is in recrimination for past sins, and when the mood of penitence gives place to the mood of relief, then the eyes are turned away from himself on others and on God.

The gift of redemption in Christ, then, is not a treasure to be savoured and delighted in like a new set of clothes. Receiving the mercy is not like winning on the football pools or the state lottery and having at one's disposal a pecuniary means of dispensing general well-being. If the saints are to be believed, it is the very reverse of suddenly being endowed with great wealth, suddenly empowered to scatter benefactions on all and sundry. It is more like being bereft of everything and knowing that it does not matter. Or, paradoxically, it is like suddenly being granted all things that have been longed for, and immediately recognising the giver of all gifts as their only source and creator. In him, through him alone can any worthwhile joy be known. That is what we learn from reading or listening to the records of men and women who have the right to speak of such matters.

There is a celebrated poem by Robert Browning, bringing to life the character of a Florentine painter, Filippo Lippi. Lippi was certainly no saint. He was a monk who abducted a nun and fathered a son. He was a painter of great zest and vitality whose work reflects a bounding delight in the world and its inhabitants. Browning portrays his imaginative vigour with great vividness. Lippi describes a painting he is planning. There will be God, the Virgin Mary and her child ringed by flowery white-faced angels, a saint or two, and Job from the Old Testament. And impinging on this scene of devotion, the painter himself will emerge from a corner, caught up to heaven in his monk's habit by some seeming blunder. Naturally, he would like to scurry away from this august company, and he seeks an escape. But a sweet young angel takes him by the hand to make him welcome. 'Not so fast,' she says. 'He made you and devised you, after all.' Moreover, the point is made that St John is no good with the painting brush.[3]

Now it is always dangerous to risk sentimentalising the picture of heaven. But the notion of being caught up by blunder into heaven, of thoroughly relishing the scene and at the same time of feeling totally unfitted to be there, smacks of a healthy spirituality. A glimpse of heavenly splendour might reasonably be expected to send the humble Christian running shamefacedly in the opposite direction in stark realisation of his unfittedness to partake of it. That seems a fair enough observation for the poet to make of the painter's attitude. Yet the resurrection life of which we are asked to partake by virtue of our Saviour's sacrifice can surely not be something which we ought politely to refuse, like a well-mannered visitor refusing the offer of cake with her cup of tea: 'Oh, no, no. Please don't bother. You mustn't go to that trouble for me.' For one thing, of course, it is too late to beg our Lord not to go to too much trouble on our behalf. He has already taken a good deal of trouble for us — if the expression may be used without irreverence of hands and feet nailed to a cross. The least we can do is to accept with gladness and gratitude what has been won for us at such cost.

The course of this argument is intended to highlight a human dilemma. If the Christian faith is true, God's own Son has died in agony on a cross so that people such as you and I need not accept as final and inescapable that miserable version of the human lot which analysis of our fallen condition presents to us. God's own Son has died in agony on a cross so that people such as you and I can escape the very sins which we feel make us unworthy to accept the proffered gift. Put like that, the idea of human unworthiness as an obstacle to acceptance of divine favour begins to sound both illogical and disrespectful. 'Lord... I am not worthy that thou shouldst enter under my roof ...but say in a word, and my servant shall be healed' (Luke 7:6–7). That was worthily said, and divinely approved of. But there is a stage at which the guest stops refusing the proffered cake. And there is a point at which the Christian stops saying, 'Lord, I am not worthy'. Indeed, if he says it too often and persistently, he might well receive the reply, 'Whoever supposed that you *were* worthy?' Christ is not offering us a prize for having borne a great burden on our pilgrimage. He is trying to remove the burden from our shoulders. We cannot logically protest that the burden makes us unworthy to have the burden removed.

There is a point in argument about matters spiritual or moral, as about matters less weighty and grave, at which common sense must be allowed to halt the course of introspective analysis, or, if not common sense, then at least the sense of humour which is generally its closest ally. In the Christian life, the corrective to excess of scruple and self-questioning is always to look away from the self to others and to God.

The Need for Grace

'Men may talk as they will, but sure there is no joy in the world to the joy of a man saved.'[4] So said Lancelot Andrewes, one of those saintly yet scholarly divines of Elizabethan and Jacobean days. He was preaching a Christmas sermon, and joy was an appropriate theme. Yet there is another aspect of life in Christ which must accompany the theme of joy as a spine accompanies the flesh it supports. For a neat summary of it let me quote a later preacher of the Restoration age, Isaac Barrow, the man who taught Isaac Newton and whose brilliance was such that at Cambridge he was successively Professor of Greek, Professor of Geometry, and Professor of Mathematics. 'Our duty moveth on this hinge, the free submission of our will to the will of God.'[5] It was this pattern, Barrow insists, which was set before us by Christ himself in the Garden of Gethsemane: 'Nevertheless not my will, but thine, be done' (Luke 22:42).

Barrow presents God's claim upon our souls as a struggle in which we must support God's assault upon our recalcitrant wills. 'We must join in the combat; *we must take the yoke upon us*; for God is only served by volunteers.'[6] This theme of the need for costly self-surrender counterpoints the theme of joy in the testimony of those best qualified to guide us. And the emphasis upon both the initiating power of God's grace and the need for willing co-operation with it is constant in Christian teaching. John Donne drew a contrast between our compulsory involvement in the fallen state and our voluntary involvement with the redeeming Christ. Not, he insisted, that our own wills contribute anything towards the attainment of eternal life, but they have a kind of negative veto which can obstruct the work of salvation.

In view of all that has been said in this book about the taming of Nature and the building of civilisation, it might be thought that the human race could achieve a great deal by the exercise of the human will in initiating invention and toil. And it might therefore seem illogical to proclaim that our only capacity for making a contribution to our spiritual renewal is the capacity to say yes or no to what is divinely initiated. But a little analysis of how the human mind and the human heart work will show how fundamental the doctrine of grace is.

The nature of the fallen human condition is such that disciplines have to be imposed on the appetites and desires. This is so at the crudest physical level for some of us. If we always eat what we feel like eating or drink what we feel like drinking, we shall put on weight, perhaps damage our liver, certainly damage our health. The natural human inclinations in that case are plainly out of key with what will benefit us. Indeed, they will lead us to destroy the basic physical well-being which is essential to contented living. We impose disciplines on our appetites, therefore. But such disciplines do not necessarily contribute to self-conquest. On the contrary, they may contribute to self-glorification. You may rigorously control your eating and drinking because your major delight in life is your own physical attractiveness, the trim figure and lithe movements which further your career as a model. You may rigorously control your eating and drinking because your ambition is to be acclaimed as a long-distance runner. We all control our desire for certain foods because we do not want to get stomach-ache. The desire for the future comfort or glorification of the self is thus a motive for restraining the appetites of the self. And it may well be that the more effectively we restrain our lower appetites, the more we shall be able to rejoice in our achievements — as model, as athlete, or as footballer of the year.

The seed of self-centred vanity and pride seems to take root in the most ostensibly worthy works we undertake. A man may exercise the most arduous self-discipline in a lifetime's toil, and yet the inner motivation may be that he should stand out among his fellows for the vastness of his industrial empire and the immensity of his wealth. A man may turn aside from the pleasures and indulgences of life to focus all his resources on making a career in politics because he longs to wield power and to see himself photographed with a ring of microphones in front of his face. A man may concentrate his efforts on forming and developing a great charitable institution for the alleviation of misery and suffering, and yet his overriding motivation may be that he should be lauded as a great philanthropist. A man may even cultivate an ingratiating manner of social self-abasement because he is determined to be known as humble and approachable. We can take pride even in our supposed humility.

What this all amounts to is that the seemingly worthiest achievements in self-discipline can be motivated more by self-centredness than by unselfishness. Moreover, efforts initially undertaken for altruistic motives, out of genuine desire to serve others, can be subtly corrupted by motives of pure self-aggrandisement and self-gratification. It would be comforting to ourselves to exemplify this by pointing our fingers at public figures who have clearly sacrificed integrity in gaining or maintaining power or influence. It would, however, be wildly wrong to imagine that statesmen, television personalities, or industrial magnates necessarily provide the best examples of this corruption. You do not need to have achieved national celebrity before you can be accused of vanity or to have acquired a private yacht before you can be accused of covetousness. At the most modest level of achievement vanity and self-gratification can erode our characters. You do not need to be a cabinet minister or a company director to take selfish pride in power. You can glorify your ego just as easily if you are a teacher in a class, a nurse at a bedside, a parson in the pulpit, or an electrician putting someone's cooker in order. As for writers, surely here they can be touched to the quick. In the old days, when Roy Plomley interviewed celebrities on his *Desert Island Discs* programme, it used to alarm me as a writer that, while distinguished musicians — even opera stars — almost always came over as modest, unpretentious, good-humoured personalities, writers all too often came over as self-important people eaten up with vanity.

Why do we press again this evidence of our fallen human nature — our susceptibility to corruption which can mar or pervert even our ostensibly most 'innocent' activities? Because we would show that there is no remedy for the despair of the fallen human condition except redemption in Christ. Indeed, the more we try to pull ourselves up by our own boot-straps, the more we open ourselves to new and subtler forms of corruption. The vanity of the swaggering show-off in the local bar or the decked-out punk in the city centre is, after all, a rather 'modest' level of vanity. Compare it with the vanity which has eaten its way into the heart of the judge who is excoriating some half-educated thief before putting him away for 10 years. Compare it with the vanity of the parson whose direction of what is supposed to be the spiritual life of his parishioners has become an opportunity for pompous self-display. On the whole, when you come to think of it, the working-class drinker in the pub and the unemployed punk in the city centre have pretty limited opportunities for self-aggrandisement compared with the judge or the parson — or with any of those whose profession opens the door to exercising influence upon others. In the extreme case, even the sermon preached against pride can be a subtle self-indulgence in pride. Indeed, the sentence just penned by the writer to make this point can be an even subtler self-indulgence in pride.

In T S Eliot's play *Murder in the Cathedral* when Thomas à Becket, Archbishop of Canterbury, faces the possibility of martyrdom at the hands of Henry II's knights, he imagines at first that the great temptation to be defeated in this struggle will be the temptation to forget his principles, come to terms with the king, and return to a life of comfort and pleasure. There will also be the temptation to believe that he can do more good by retaining his position of earthly authority and power, and using it for the public weal, than by dying. He recognises the pull of self-service in these temptations and resists them. But then he is surprised to find a more insidious temptation still facing him at the last — the temptation to go forward to martyrdom, taking pride in the ultimate achievement of sanctity — in the thought of glory after death, of a martyr's shrine, and of pilgrims queuing before it in search of miraculous help.

> The last temptation is the greatest treason:
> To do the right deed for the wrong reason.[7]

There is nothing on earth, even the act of martyrdom it-self, which cannot be corrupted in the service of human pride. Thus, the more deeply we analyse our moral con-dition, the more we human beings seem to be trapped in a labyrinth from which the unaided self can never escape to selflessness.

There is no escape by earthly self-discipline, by moral education, by altruistic striving towards the service of others. There is no escape from the fact that the fabric of our achievements may be worm-eaten within by pride and self-gratification. This does not mean, of course, that you might just as well satisfy your vanity by robbing a bank as by raising a vast sum for Oxfam. It does mean that the man who raises the sum for Oxfam may be seen by virtue of his basic motivation in a not very different spiritual light from the man who robs the bank. These points need to be stressed because there is an idea abroad today that current ills in society could be remedied by a return to something called 'Victorian val-ues'. This appears to amount to a general exhortation to people to exercise more self-reliance, independence, and initiative, to use their own ingenuity and cultivate the capacity for hard work. But, of course, all these qual-ities — self-reliance, independence, initiative, ingenu-ity and hard work — have marked the careers of master-criminals as well as of great industrialists. All these qualities may be manifested in building up an entre-preneurial business that exploits the weakest to line the pockets of the few. And to exhort to the exercise of these qualities youngsters who can find no legitimate employment for their hands or their talents is sheer hypocrisy. If they respond by taking the advice literally, and use initiative and ingenuity to make money by smuggling and marketing drugs, they may find themselves punished by the establishment which encouraged them.

There is no non-Christian remedy for the malaise of the fallen human condition. And this is so for the very good reason that the more things are given to a human being, whether it be by way of wealth or power, education or health, culture or influence, the more opportunities for corruption are supplied. Every new acquisition, whether it be a possession or a talent, a function or a status, is another means of potential corruption. The redemption offered in Christ is not an ultimate achievement, setting the crown on all other earthly achievements. It is the end of achieving and the beginning of being used. Salvation in Christ is not the ultimate acquisition by which all previous acquisitions are consummated and transcended. Salvation in Christ is the end of acquiring and the beginning of receiving.

It is not easy for us, whose minds have been conditioned to conceive of earthly life in terms of acquiring and achieving, to conceive of a climactic fulfilment which violates the pattern of acquisition and achievement instead of consummating it. We more naturally conceive of the ultimate happiness as 'All this and heaven too'. We want to keep our health and vigour, our family and loved ones, our talents and gifts, our enjoyments and delights in nature, in art, in music, in books, in walking, in swimming.... We want to keep all these and add that final touch of felicity, the knowledge of God's favour and the prospect of permanently relishing what we have through all eternity. Certainly the saints assure us that in Christ all things worth having are restored to us, and there is no doubt that the list of blessings we have given are worth having. Nevertheless, our Lord's own words require us to lose our lives in order to save our souls. And this demand represents a break with all our previous notions of achievement. We have conceived of the ultimate happiness in terms of getting something that will set the crown on all acquisitions and achievements. We have not faced up to the fact that salvation in Christ is a gift of different category from all other gifts. We cling to the illusion that there is a crucial difference between regretting what we lack today and boasting of what we possess tomorrow, between bemoaning our ill-fortune today and crowing over our good fortune tomorrow. But there is no such antithesis. The moods of regret for what we have not got and of pride for all we have got are rooted in the same acquisitiveness. Do we realise what this means? It means that advertising your own salvation to the world may not after all be essentially different in its moral category from advertising your own sinfulness to the world. The opposite of humble penitence is not pride in salvation: it is forgiveness. To be penitent is to ask; to be forgiven is to have received. The receiver looks at the giver, as the asker looks at the benefactor.

From all that has been said, it should be clear that the Christian's consciousness of the Fall is not a matter of accepting some ancient myth or even some historic truth which, once accepted, can be treated as a bulwark by which our faith is buttressed; for the Fall is an issue of ever-present relevance. The Christian's understanding of the Fall is his understanding of contemporary civilisation, of what is happening all around him in the public sphere and in the private sphere, and, indeed, of what is happening within him. Correspondingly, the Christian's consciousness of redemption is not simply a matter of accepting the Gospel records as reliable, of knowing cerebrally that Christ was the Son of God, that he died to pay the price of human sinfulness and to open up to us all the way of salvation. The Christian's understanding of redemption can never be fully defined in terms of events that happened long ago, however important or influential. The Christian's understanding of redemption is as much an aspect of his outlook upon the world today as an element in his historical knowledge. If the doctrine of the Fall explains what kind of a world we live in, the doctrine of redemption tells us how to cope with that situation. Or rather — for 'tells us how to cope' represents but the feeblest beginning of the work of redeeming love — the fact of redemption embraces us in the company of those who are called out of the fallen world, are lifted out of the fallen world. 'I have given them thy word,' our Lord said of his disciples in the High Priestly prayer, 'and the world hath hated them, because they are not of the world, even as I am not of the world' (John 17:14). The contrast between 'the world' and the condition of the chosen saved is pressed home:

> I pray not that thou shouldest take them out of the world, but that thou shouldest keep them from the evil. They are not of the world, even as I am not of the world. Sanctify them through thy truth; thy word is truth. As thou hast sent me into the world, even so have I also sent them into the world.
>
> (John 17:15–18)

The Role of the Chosen

The chosen are sent into the world. They are to be in the

world but not of the world. To be in the world and not of
the world is to be hated by the world. Our Lord's prayer
takes in the destiny not only of those he sends immediately, but 'them also which shall believe on me through
their word' (John 17:20). So the message which recognises that the saved will be at loggerheads with their
world is more than a message to Jews who have self-
righteous, pedantic Pharisees to deal with, mercenary
publicans, the hangers-on of Herod Antipas, the Roman
legionaries, and the Procurator Pilate. It is also a message
to those who have heretical bishops and atheistical
school-teachers to tackle, newspaper editors who steadily decompose the moral standards of their readers, and
all other sponsors of erosive permissiveness. In so far as
they are of the world, those claiming a share in the
redemptive grace will be at war with them. We must not
expect that those who are 'of the world' and therefore
Christ's enemies will all wear the outer uniform of criminality. Perhaps there are plenty of squalid drug-
pushers, vicious murderers, brutal muggers, and other
seeming riff-raff of our civilisation among them. But the
apostle of 'caring' who would destroy the family out of
compassion for the sexually indisciplined is of their
company too. And the wealthy manipulator of commod-
ity shortages who plays the market is one with them also.
So is the academic who pushes Marxist propaganda
under the 'freedom of speech' banner, while opposing
Christian commitment as antithetic to 'freedom of
enquiry'. As for the father-in-God who uses his status
and authority to corrupt the faith of those he is ordained
to nourish in the truth, what can we say of him, except
that it may be better to have a millstone round your neck
than a mitre on your head?

The world from which the saved are called to be distinct

is not just the world of obvious criminality and corruption. For we have seen how the apostles of post-Christian secularism have begun a take-over of those nourishing agencies of our civilisation, such as education and the media, which ought to be utilised in the service of men and women as God's children. The world from which the saved are called to be distinct is not a world alive with people who say to themselves: 'In spite of God's law, I'm going to have this, or that'; 'In spite of God's claim upon me, I'm going to have my own way'; 'In spite of God's prescript against adultery, I'm going to run off with my neighbour's wife'. Our task as Christians would be much simpler if the world were amok with people claiming that God's ordinances are too hard for them to keep, God's will for them too demanding to be obeyed. There may have been times and places in the history of Christendom at which believers had to deal with disobedience to God by rebels who consciously flouted his word. Nowadays, however, the world is alive with people to whom no appeal can be made in terms of God's law and their disobedience, for they do not believe in God. They do not allow for a God in the scheme of things. Worse still, as we shall see later, they have taken over the vocabulary of virtue and love, mercy and compassion, and utilise it in defence of practices which God's law forbids and in corroboration of attitudes which eliminate God from his world. Compassion for lesbian partners requires that they should be allowed to bring up a child in their 'family'. Compassion for members of ethnic communities with Muslim or other religious affiliations requires us to bring up our own children without instruction in Christianity.

The prophets and leaders of the world are perhaps never so dangerously corrupting to Christians as when

they assume a 'Christian' vesture. The philosophy of the
world is perhaps never so insidiously erosive of the
Christian mind as when it ostensibly seeks to further
open-ended tolerance and denigrate doctrinal firmness.
It is fatally easy in our current mental climate to smear
credal assurance which will have no truck with heresy
as 'bigoted', 'closed-minded', 'inflexible', and 'narrow'.
It is even fashionable to apply words such as 'outgoing',
'adventurous', 'positive', 'courageous', and (alas, alas)
'creative' to people who challenge Christian orthodoxy,
and conversely to suggest that the defenders of the faith
are 'frightened' and 'negative' seekers after 'cosiness'
and 'shelter'. Yet anyone who thinks rationally about
our current intellectual climate will recognise that it is
laughably absurd to pretend that it requires either courage or originality to cotton on to the anti-orthodox
temper of the times and repeat the slogans and clichés of
the now established conventionalism of supposed un-
conventionality.

Creeping worldliness insinuates itself as damagingly
by subtly corrupting the mind with the false values of
secularised modernity as by plainly corrupting the heart
with covetousness or greed. It is at work in the Church
when a bishop, seemingly moved by compassion for the
victims of Nazi atrocities, proclaims that God's failure to
halt these bestial cruelties by miraculous intervention
renders absurd the notion that he could have raised
Christ physically from the dead. The gist of the case
appears to be that since God neither prevented the
United States Air Force from dropping atom bombs on
Hiroshima and Nagasaki, nor prevented the Nazi SS
from massacring Jews in Belsen and Auschwitz, he cannot with consistency abandon his non-intervention policy over such lesser individual matters as raising any

Tom, Dick, or Lazarus — let alone a Jesus — from the
dead. By his choice of words, the Bishop tries to give to
individual biblical miracles a quality of 'vulgarity' from
which the deeply thoughtful or sensitive mind would re-
coil:

> We are faced with the claim that God is pre-
> pared to work knock-down physical miracles
> in order to let a select number of people into
> the secret of his incarnation, resurrection and
> salvation but he is not prepared to use such
> methods in order to deliver from Auschwitz,
> prevent Hiroshima, overcome famine or bring
> about a bloodless transformation of
> apartheid.[8]

God is God, and what he is allowed or not allowed to
do does not have to be determined by any of his bishops.
This chapter is an attempt to explore the nature of
redemption and the mystery of salvation. Whatever else
being saved may involve, it can never possibly put you
in the position of being able to tell God his business. The
whole divine revelation operates to other ends than
nourishing Christians to the point at which they can in-
struct God on what is theologically appropriate for him
to do, and can define what acts would conflict with the
divine character we have graciously assigned to him.

Nevertheless, the Bishop's argument involves this
astounding claim:

> If God is this sort of loving, identifying and
> gracious God, then surely we must be very
> careful, reverent and reticent when we pin
> certain sorts of miracles to him. The choice of

physical miracles with what might be called laser-beam-like precision and power would, I suggest, not seem to be a choice which he cared or would care to use.[9]

The crux of this argument is that *we* must be careful about what acts *we* choose to pin on God. And the conclusion rests on the view that raising the dead, healing the blind, and feeding the 5,000 'would not seem to be a choice which he cared or would care to use'. The Bishop's argument thus scraps the Christian revelation on which the faith of the Church has always rested. The basis of the case is essentially one from which faith has been excluded in favour of what *we* think a God might care or not care to do. G S Hood in an earlier article in *The Times* (March 29th, 1986) headed 'Resurrection of Body and Soul' quickly got to the heart of the matter:

> It is also fashionable to wonder whether the Resurrection narratives were meant to be taken literally. That is the viewpoint of someone on the outside looking in, for the Church is a continuous and continuing body, and those inside it have an unbroken tradition of the meaning of those narratives.

The Bishop's viewpoint is that of 'someone on the outside looking in'. It discards all the Christian perspectives. It is alarming because it embraces secularist anti-supernaturalist prejudices on the subject of the miraculous and gives them priority over the testimony of the evangelists and the living faith of the Church.

The Church of England has always had its misguided and heretical clergy. What many Christians will find even more disturbing than the Bishop's statement, therefore, is surely the sympathetic public response it elicited from a large section of the synodical audience. A besetting failing of many people, even people who pride themselves on their independence, is that they will treat clichés or shallow arguments seriously and gravely if they are uttered by men and women of external status and authority. Among the English, this failing is related perhaps to that class-consciousness which, according to those overseas, helps to give the UK its anachronistic organisational inefficiency. There may be something in this theory. Certainly class-consciousness would cause most English people to listen respectfully to a duke, even if what he had to say was scarcely worth hearing. It is, however, quite out of keeping with Christian integrity to treat questionable utterances from the mouth of a bishop as they would not be treated from the mouth of an insignificant layman. Errors which would be rightly and quickly countered and corrected in young students by a sound teacher ought not to be dignified with reverent attention because they are boldly proclaimed in Synod from the episcopal bench.

This discreditable episode is relevant to our case because it shows how complex is the task of defining the boundary of 'the world' in our own society, a boundary which must be recognised if we are to fulfil our Lord's injunction. For, clearly, an ecclesiastical body becomes essentially an agency of 'the world' if secularist presuppositions or questions of social and academic status assert themselves with such priority that judgement in Christian terms is laid aside, and an attack upon the Christian faith is applauded. In short, here is a striking example of the way in which 'the world' corrupts the Church, and of the way in which professing Christians,.

in a moment of sudden challenge, choose to be 'of the world' as well as in it.

There are times, indeed, when Church of England clergy seem to strive to outdo the world itself in 'worldliness' in respect of this matter of veneration of those who have achieved worldly status or fame. If press reports are to be trusted, then at the memorial service in Westminster Abbey for the poet Philip Larkin, an avowed atheist, a dignitary praised Larkin's integrity for not accepting the consolations of the faith he could not share. Now there is no record of Christ or any of the apostles having commended lack of faith as 'integrity'. A thousand quotations could be assembled to corroborate a very different view. The clerical tribute in this case reached an almost parodic level in the determination to be on the world's side: 'He now shares our rejoicing in eternal life, the gift of the risen Christ he did not know.'[10] Indeed, we *hope* that such is the case for him and for every human soul, however fraught with infidelities his pilgrimage. But, clearly, no riest of the Church ought to speak thus. The matter is noted here because it seems to bring together two insidious lines of corruption. The one is the desire to swing the authority of the Church behind what is culturally valued by 'the world', even to the extent of turning Christian beliefs topsy-turvy. The other is the secularist challenge to Christian teaching implicit in the tacit declaration to God: 'We admire this atheistic integrity. We defy you to be less broad-minded than we are.'

If we are seeking to understand more clearly what the pattern of life should be for those who claim to be in the company of the redeemed, we should observe that our Lord's prayer that his disciples should be in the world and not of the world follows upon an initial declaration which parallels what they have to do with what he himself has done. Our Lord declares that he has glorified the Father on earth and finished the work the Father gave him to do (John 17:4). He has manifested the Father's name to the disciples given him 'out of the world' (John 17:6). The disciples know that whatever has been granted to him has been granted by God the Father. They have had the Father's own message conveyed to them through Christ. The emphasis is upon the assurance of the disciples' understanding that what is of Christ is of God, that his teaching is God's teaching, that his call is God's call. And Christ's concern is that when he leaves the earthly scene, the disciples whom he has protected by the power given to him by God, should then in his absence be protected directly by the power of the Father.

The parallel drawn between our Lord's purpose in the world and the future role of his disciples is a close one. Before the Crucifixion, God's act in initiating the process of redemption is made plain. He gave the Son a task to perform, or, since he and his Son are one, he came himself. It was a case of setting the divine life in the human neighbourhood. (I borrow a phrase from Austin Farrer's *Saving Belief*.[11]) In a sense there can never be any other Christian duty than that, to set the divine life in the human neighbourhood.

Christ's Coming Among Us

What it meant to set the divine life in the human neighbourhood can be gathered from the Gospels. What the consequences were of setting the divine life in the human neighbourhood can also be gathered from the Gospels. Our Lord drew a group of disciples about him. He taught them privately and he taught others publicly. He moved among people of every social class. When they appealed for help in sickness or infirmity, he healed them. When they lamented their loss in bereavement, at least on some occasions he restored their dead to life (with a total disregard for episcopal prohibitions). He expounded the Scriptures in the synagogue. No life could have been more innocently, more philanthropically, more helpfully spent; yet he was killed for it. It is true that when gross abuses and hypocrisies were presented to his eyes, he did not spare the lash of his tongue. Moreover, he did not suffer from any ingrained inhibitions, making him tolerant of nonsense when it issued from the lips of those holding lofty ecclesiastical office. Yet he can scarcely be said to have challenged the civil or ecclesiastical establishment in such a way that it was compelled to eliminate him.

In our own day we may observe of some tyrant or bully, some self-inflated paranoid, perhaps of quite modest status by profession and achievement, that what gets under his skin most acutely is not the excited hostility of overt critics and judges of his ways, but the silence and seemingly tranquil equability of some quite undemonstrative man or woman. The quiet, unassertive individual scarcely breathes a word or even a sigh in the face of the bully's tantrums, but his very presence, serene and unruffled, seems to represent a challenge to all postures and pretensions. Now our Lord did not always remain silent and equable when the shallow postures of the proud confronted him. Nevertheless, the sheer distinctiveness of his manner, the unfussy confidence in his own authority, the thoroughness of his good will to the responsive, and the direct simplicity of his call to repentance seem to have turned him into an abrasive irritant to those who boosted themselves as office-holders and feathered their nests by sustaining the status quo.

It can be spiritually perilous to seek close parallels between our Lord's ways of dealing with a wicked world and what we ourselves are called upon to do. It is better to find examples for our own instruction in the responses of those whom he called directly to his service, or of those whom he turned aside to comfort, befriend, or cleanse. What was it like to run into Jesus at the end of the street or at the door of the temple? There were, of course, those who encountered him with an urgent demand, who were desperately looking for help, and in these cases the initiative was taken by the suppliant. A ruler rushes up to prostrate himself at Jesus' feet and to announce that his daughter is at the point of death (Matt 9:18); a woman tugs at his robe because she is suffering from a chronic haemorrhage (Matt 8:20); a centurion approaches him declaring that his servant is ill and dying (Matt 8:5, 6). In such cases our Lord puts those who appeal to him out of their misery with seemingly very little fuss and no great pressure of exhortation. But there were chance meetings with our Lord, too, on the part of people who did not seek him out for aid in desperate need. There was the woman of Samaria, for whom the encounter brought an unravelling of her past (John 4:5–26). And there was Zacchaeus, for whom the encounter brought a different kind of unravelling of his past.

The story of Zacchaeus (Luke 19:1–10) is indeed one of the most fascinating in the New Testament. Here is a rich tax-gatherer who, it appears, from sheer curiosity thinks he would like to get a good view of this man Jesus when he walks through Jericho. And being a short fellow, and finding the street crowded with spectators also wanting a glimpse of Jesus, he climbs up into a tree to get a better view. Jesus spots him there, immediately tells him to get down, and invites himself to lunch. Zacchaeus receives the celebrity cheerfully enough; but what a costly bit of entertaining it turns out to be for him! The Gospel account is terse and simple. There is no analysis of a change of mood on Zacchaeus' part. There is nothing but pure hard fact. Christ invites himself to lunch and it is not long before Zacchaeus is signing away half his capital and promising to pay four times over for any excess of overcharging in the past. Whatever the current rate of inflation, this sounds to be generous recompense. Outside there is general murmuring among the crowd that Christ has chosen odd company for a meal, but the host is meanwhile standing before the uninvited guest and saying, 'Behold, Lord, the half of my goods I give to the poor; and if I have taken anything from any man by false accusation, I restore him fourfold' (Luke 19:8). Christ is as crisp and decisive as Zacchaeus himself. 'This day is salvation come to this house' (Luke 19:9) he declares and, presumably, walks out of the door waving a massive cheque made out to poor relief. The moral would seem to point to the worldly unwisdom of trying to get too close to our Lord. It also indicates the drastic developments which can take place when our Lord gets his foot inside the door of a home and is received at its table.

It is one of Samuel Beckett's characters whose gloom about life leads him to the conclusion that the raising of Lazarus was the 'one occasion on which the Saviour overstepped the mark'. It might be argued that the words spoken at the door of Zacchaeus' dwelling, 'This day is salvation come to this house', smack of divine understatement in view of the extent to which the owner's bank balance has been depleted.

Do we really want to have our Lord in our home declaring

that salvation has come to it, if it means signing away half our resources to Oxfam or Christian Aid? There would seem to be something to be said for keeping salvation at a distance, if that is a fair measure of its market price. And there would also seem to be something to be said for not climbing into too prominent a place when our Lord is due to pass by. It might be wiser to keep one's head down.

Perhaps it is as well that we know so little about Zacchaeus. Was he a married man? If so, was his wife involved in his extravagant gesture; or did he have to explain it to her as best he could when she came home? Had he any children? And if he had, were they the kind to have calculated in advance what they might stand to inherit on his decease? Was there further explaining to be done at the next family gathering in father's home? What were the concrete consequences of carving up the domestic nest-egg and distributing it among needy paupers and cheated taxpayers? Were there projected holidays to be cancelled, proposed home improvements to be called off, a cut to be made in the regular supplies from the grocers and the vintners? There is so little detail in the story of the kind which brings a human situation vividly to life before us. Just a man giving his treasure away; and we have to draw our own conclusions. Whether the officers of the Inland Revenue were a sufficiently cohesive or organised body for Zacchaeus' action to send ripples of consternation and anger through the hearts of his colleagues we are not told. Might there have been a union chapel meeting at which Zacchaeus' imprudence and folly were censured, a threat to withdraw his membership debated, and a warning given against any comparable misdemeanours by others? Was a message of condolence sent by the branch secretary to his wife? Did the bank manager request an interview just to make sure that so large a payment was indeed intended, and that the celebrity had not forged his signature? Did his accountant shake his head in dismay over the falling figures in his ledger? Did tradesmen become apprehensive as rumours of Zacchaeus' rash munificence spread? Did Rent-a-Chariot send in the quarterly account prematurely just to make sure? Did friends and neighbours whisper together at street corners about the growing eccentricities of Zacchaeus the revenue-man? Was it hinted to Mrs Zacchaeus that a session with a psychiatrist might do her husband the world of good?

It is pleasant to indulge these speculations. Pleasant to let the mind wander over what happened in Jericho long ago. Much pleasanter than concentrating too strenuously on the simple given fact, unembroidered by detail, untouched by local colour, that a middle-class professional man of means took our Lord into his house and promptly reversed the habits of a lifetime. He ran his hand through his hair, asked himself, 'What can I do?', then cheerfully reached for his stylus and handed over half his money for the needy.

We are not tempted to compete with Zacchaeus. We shall never by such acts as his deserve to have that notice stuck over our doorway: 'This day is salvation come to this house.'

Was it really necessary for the divine plan to redeem mankind to involve this kind of thing? Somehow it seems a long way from proclaiming the master-plan for the salvation of mankind to the assembled hosts in the courts of heaven to sitting down to lunch with a rather unscrupulous taxman, tweaking his conscience, twisting his arm, and then congratulating him for being ready to make amends to all those whose code-numbers he had falsified. 'Setting the divine life in the human neighbourhood' sounds like a fine way of rescuing mankind. In the abstract, it suggests a human neighbourhood suddenly ennobled by the presence of divinity, exalted in the light of heaven itself. In the concrete, it seems to boil down sometimes to pretty humdrum encounters with rather seedy personalities, even to slumming it with alcoholics, harlots, and drop-outs. It is less taxing to contemplate 'the divine life in the human neighbourhood' in general terms without getting down to brass tacks, or to the nitty-gritty, as we say today. The Light of the World, crowned and robed, standing at the door awaiting admission, has a grandeur and pathos which, we feel, can perhaps best be preserved by keeping him there. The Light of the World getting his legs under the table at lunch time is a different persona. To begin with, it would presumably be polite to remove the crown when eating.

He was not wearing his crown when he called on Zacchaeus. And there was clearly none of the embarrassment that would have been caused in the household had the Light of the World turned up as Holman Hunt pictured him. The problem is that talk of 'setting the divine life in the human neighbourhood' somehow still distances our Lord. We would rather have him in the neighbourhood than at the door. And we would rather have him at the door than at the lunch table. For it appears that it is when he gets firmly inside the place that the trouble really starts. Promises are apt to be made, and they have to be kept.

How exactly did Zacchaeus fulfil his promise? We shall have to leave to the scholars the question of how the bureaucracy operated and what implements they used in the days of Herod the Tetrarch. We can but conceive of what the fulfilling of Zacchaeus' promise would mean in terms of our own world. Presumably, he would have to communicate by circular to all past tax-payers on his list, enclosing a pro-forma to be filled in by applicants wishing to claim compensation for this or that year ending the fifth or fifteenth of April. The keeping of the promise might well have been an onerous as well as an expensive business.

All this follows from sitting down at table with the Light of the World. No wonder Holman Hunt's picture which kept him knocking at the door proved so popular. For we are trying to make the point that the entry of Christ into the innermost recesses of home and of heart is likely to turn things topsy-turvy. There is a story of how, when the poet Tennyson had settled in his home at Farringford in the Isle of Wight, there was a knock at the door one morning, and it turned out to be Prince Albert, calling informally to ask whether he might bring the Queen round to see him. The royal visit was made. And we tend to picture the occasion of royal condescension in images of the sovereign's arrival at the door, the gracious bowing and curtseying and greeting. It is harder to picture, say, the scene in the hall when the issue becomes a matter of which hook to hang the Prince's hat on and which to hang the Queen's cloak on, or the scene in the sitting-room when seats have to be assigned and possibly a spare one fetched from another room to accommodate a lady-in-waiting. As for the business of handing cups of coffee round and plastering the right amount of anchovy paste on the royal slice of bread, these details somehow detract from the magnificent dignity of the occasion. Stately condescension can so easily degenerate into crude everyday matiness if someone upsets a cup of coffee, or a lady-in-waiting whispers to her hostess that Her Majesty would like to pop up to the bathroom.

'Thou didst leave thy throne and thy kingly crown when thou camest to earth for me' runs a once popular hymn.[12] The emphasis on what our Lord has done for us is healthy enough; but the story of Zacchaeus is a striking instance of how we are expected to respond, of what receiving him into our homes and hearts amounts to. Of course, it represents only one side of our Lord's ministry, the private side. That kind of thing turns individual lives upside-down, but it scarcely represents a threat to the powers-that-be. A person may go around getting individuals, even responsible bureaucrats, to repent their misdeeds and reform their ways without upsetting the establishment. But our Lord did not content himself with such interference in private lives. There may have been no crown on his head and no sceptre in his hand, but he spoke publicly of his kingdom and his kingship. The contrast is a sharp one, the contrast between hob-nobbing with wine-bibbers and sinners, having lunch with an extortionate revenue-man, and chivvying Martha of Bethany about the housework on the one hand, and on the other hand, proclaiming the coming of the Kingdom. This latter, of course, was what offended the ecclesiastical and, indeed, the civil authorities of the day. It would appear that, if our Lord's entry into our private lives is perhaps going to be costly in personal material terms, his enrolment of us under his public banner is unlikely to make us popular with the powers-that-be, and is perhaps going to get us into hot water with them.

There is after all something to be said for Holman Hunt's picture of the crowned Christ knocking at the door. Sovereigns do not, by and large, go round knocking on people's doors. Queen Victoria's condescension to Tennyson was so noteworthy that biographers have recorded it as an instance of signal honour paid to a great man. God's very presence on earth in Christ was a prolonged royal condescension. Yet to speak of it thus may be misleading. To suggest that God's sovereignty in itself keeps him aloof from his world and that only in exceptional circumstances would he involve himself in its day-to-day affairs is to misconceive God's sovereignty. The story of Zacchaeus, like many other biblical stories, testifies to God's continuing personal involvement on the human scene.

People who live under a constitutional monarchy are accustomed to pay their respects to a sovereign whose duty it is not to interfere. On the pattern of this national sovereignty there is a temptation to turn God into a constitutional monarch who does not interfere. God is not a constitutional divinity. No doubt there are theologians who would like to turn him into a constitutional God who, if he keeps the rules of the game, will never interfere. They would urge him not to lower himself to the mundane level of miracle-monger. The role of the constitutional God confines him to less vulgarly spectacular activities. Raising the dead is out, along with changing water into wine and striking cathedral towers with lightning. As the constitutional earthly monarch keeps above the practical political fray and exercises no influence at all on decision making in parliament, so the constitutional God sits enthroned in eternity above the mundane doings of this world. All he is allowed to do is to give formal official approval to decisions made by synods, signing their adopted resolutions on the dotted line.

It has become customary in the United Kingdom for

people to nod their heads in sympathy over photographs of the Queen about her royal duties and to say, 'I wouldn't have her job for anything'. Indeed, there is much about the monarch's role which looks unenviable. The comments of her subjects, the criticisms sometimes aired, and above all the uncongenial character of some of the ministers which the system imposes upon her as advisers, arouse sympathy for her over the burden she bears. And it is difficult to avoid being stirred to sympathy with God for the burden he bears as he listens (if he does listen) to people telling him what he can and cannot properly do. The role of constitutional God would indeed be a taxing one. Fortunately, however, God is not a constitutional God. He has no need to leak his preferences and dislikes through moles and spokesmen. His will has been made known through the prophets and the evangelists, the saints and martyrs.

Epiphanies

The Christian faith is faith in a God who has made himself known. It is faith in a God who has spoken, acted, and intervened; who has not only cared for but has visited his people. No one can read about the saints of the past or come into contact with the saints of the present without recognising that God continues to visit his people. We do not live in a forsaken world. It is a world in which on any day the hand of God may be revealed to us. This can be said without in any way throwing a cloak of verbal sentimentality over real grief and calamity. The morning brings bright sunshine. Midday brings news of 170 miners killed in a South African gold mine. That is the world we live in. Small wonder that it can be explained only by the seemingly incongruous notion of a God who both created its beauties and endured its agonies. Here a child dies of cancer at the age of nine; there a child is brutally murdered at the age of six. That is the world we live in. God entered into it himself, enduring the worst of its brutalities; a stoning, a trial, a mocking, a scourging, and a crucifixion. If faith can make anything at all of the mining disaster, surely it is that these miners' bodies were not the first to be entombed, and that on one occasion, anyway, a stone was rolled away and a body restored to life.

The themes of Christian teaching are like life itself: they hurtle between the poles of suffering and joy, sacrifice and fulfilment. When our Lord blessed the wine and said, 'This is my blood' (Matt 26:28; Mark 14:24) he drew attention to the way a victim was slaughtered, and its blood made sacrificially efficacious. What Christ consecrated was a body which was to be broken and blood which was to be shed. And yet that sacrifice was paradoxically to be the means of joyfully accomplishing the divine purpose. If the Last Supper speaks of the coming sacrifice, there are other references in our Lord's teaching to feastings of a different kind, where the Bridegroom will gather his guests joyfully around him.

It is always more congenial for the writer to dwell on what is delightful than on what is saddening. But every book has its own proper substance. Our initial theme was that the life around us is littered with evidence of the Fall. We might have taken a very different starting-point. The theme might have been that human life is littered with evidence of God's lovingly creative hand upon it. Indeed, it so happens that I have recently published a book on this very subject, *The Marks of the Maker*[13] (in the USA published as *Words Made Flesh*[14]). It is specifically designed to display in detail how much that we see around us in our world and in our fellow human beings speaks revealingly of our Creator's wisdom, power, and splendour.

The Maker's fingerprints are all about us. I write this paragraph in the season of Epiphany. The feast of the Epiphany has become traditionally associated in the Western Church with the manifestation of Christ to the Gentiles that occurred when the three Magi brought their gifts of gold, frankincense, and myrrh to the child Jesus. But in the East it was first recognised as a celebration recalling Christ's baptism. Among the cluster of associations now gathered round the feast are Christ's first miracle at the wedding feast and the discovery of the boy Jesus in the temple. References to these occasions are found in Epiphany hymns. All are revelatory events which proclaimed Christ's divinity to the world.

An interesting extension of the use of the word 'epiphany' has been made in books about literature. Writers are often concerned to fasten on to momentary experiences in life which suddenly strike them with the force of a revelation. In this sense we all have memories of private 'epiphanies'. For the Christian, life is littered with minor epiphanies which ever so slightly lift the corner of the curtain veiling the Creator at his work. Many of them seem too slight to record, yet the strands they weave into life's pattern are particularly colourful. It may be a few words from a friend or a preacher that stick in the mind, the sight of a surprisingly lovely sunset after rain, or even a near miss on the road at a dangerous junction. Cheerful, or disturbing, the event reminds us briefly how we stand under God's oversight.

On that crucial Epiphany, St John the Baptist recognised our Lord and the destiny that overhung him: 'Behold the Lamb of God, which taketh away the sin of the world' (John 1:29). Christ was recognised as the lamb without blemish whose sacrificial blood would win pardon from judgement. Last spring I was stopped one day in my walk by the sound of a lamb's bleating. I found one caught in a fence half-way between the field and the road. Naturally I freed it, pulling it through and then dropping it back into the field. Now if there had been a ewe about, no doubt that would have been the end of the matter. The lamb would have been called promptly away from the interfering biped. But there was no ewe about. The lamb decided that it had found a friend and also a way of getting at him. It wriggled through the fence again to enjoy my company. I repeatedly put it back in the field, but every touch strengthened the bond between us. It got out again and again, and worse still, when I made a sudden dash to sprint for home it skipped gaily after me. A man does not care to arrive home for tea with a lamb at his heels. It smacks of the nursery school. And ringing up local farmers with the information that a lost lamb could be reclaimed at our door would surely make me look foolish. Fortunately, I eventually found a patch of field protected by an impenetrable stretch of fence: I dropped the lamb inside and ran quickly home without looking behind me.

This little 'epiphany' reminded me how God has been pictured as the divine Hound of Heaven chasing his human quarry through life, determined to catch and claim him. Perhaps the image of the Hound is unnecessary. Apparently a lamb, once approached by a human being, is just as likely to pursue the new-found acquaintance. We cannot get away from the sound of the following feet by picturing the divine Lamb instead of the divine Hound. Nevertheless, it is not terrifying to be chased by a lamb; rather it is embarrassing. And this makes the little 'epiphany' especially revelatory. In our day we are less likely to feel the divine demand upon us to be a threat and more likely to feel it to be an embarrassment. If an evangelist stands up like St Paul in your local market-place to preach Christ crucified, no listener will blench in terror or run away in fear; but many might turn aside in embarrassment. The message is a message of love and a call to penitence. To be confronted with it is to be chased by a lamb, and that hurts one's dignity.

When a Chancellor of the Exchequer in the House of Commons wanted to mock the weakness of the Opposition spokesman's attack on his Budget speech, he said that he felt as though he had been 'savaged by a sheep'. The Christian's lot is to be chased by a Lamb and to be overtaken by a Lamb. It is also to have his pride and self-centredness savaged by a Lamb.

Notes

1 F L Cross (ed), *The Oxford Dictionary of the Christian Church* (Oxford University Press: London, 1957).
2 Charlotte Brontë, *Jane Eyre* (Penguin: London, 1971 [first published 1847]), p 474.
3 Robert Browning, 'Fra Lippo Lippi', *Men and Women, Browning: Poetical Works, 1883–1864* (Oxford University Press: London, 1970), p 568.
4 Quoted from: G Lacey May (ed), *Wings of an Eagle: An Anthology of Caroline Preachers* (SPCK: London, 1955).
5 G Lacey May, *ibid*.
6 G Lacey May, *ibid*.
7 T S Eliot, *Murder in the Cathedral*, *Collected Plays*

(Faber and Faber: London, 1962), p 30.

8   The Bishop of Durham, The Rt Rev David Jenkins, addressing the Church of England Synod, *The Times* (July 7th, 1986).

9   The Bishop of Durham, *ibid*.

10 Frederick Shail, *The Winchester Churchman* (June, 1986).

11 Austin Farrer, *Saving Belief: A Discussion of Essentials* (Hodder and Stoughton: London, 1964).

12 Emily Elizabeth Steele Elliot, 'Thou didst leave thy throne and thy kingly crown', *Hymns of Faith* (Scripture Union: London, 1964).

13 Harry Blamires, *The Marks of the Maker* (Kingsway Publications: Eastbourne, 1987).

14 Harry Blamires, *Words Made Flesh* (Servant Books: Ann Arbor, Michigan, 1985).

4
Counter–Christianity and the Alternative Ethic

The Ethic of Obedience

Because Christianity is a religion of revelation, of God's will made known in history, it follows that the moral keynote of Christianity must be obedience. Believers who hold that God's purpose has been unfolded for them have no rational choice except to fit in with it. We have already made the point that in the contemporary world the young are less likely to be brought up to conceive of life as presenting them with moral and cultural frameworks to which they must accommodate themselves than to be brought up to conceive of life as presenting them with moral and cultural frameworks which have to be destroyed in the name of self-realisation and self-fulfilment. A picture of life is being painted for the young which suggests that personal development and personal fulfilment are a matter of asserting the undisciplined ego and indulging its whims with scorn of traditional restraints and established codes. Progress is envisaged in terms of the continuing expansion of a process of personal liberation from historically imposed conventions and restrictions.

Here, indeed, the confrontation between secularist and Christian thinking is one of total antagonism. The moral keynote of Christianity is obedience. From the testing of Abraham with Isaac to the rescue of Noah from the Flood, from the angelic annunciation to the Virgin Mary to our Lord's calling of St Peter the human role has been represented as that of obedience. God calls and man obeys. The divine process of rescuing mankind from sin and death was initiated when the Virgin Mary said, 'Be it unto me according to thy word' (Luke 1:38). This represented a total surrender of the human spirit, the human mind, the human body, to the will of God. The Virgin Mary did not reply, 'Let me think about it.' Nor did she reply 'The female body is not a piece of reproductive machinery; it is a source of strength, pride, and pleasure; and it is mine. I cannot bargain it away in exchange for the dubious privilege of motherhood. I detect a subtle divine pressure to make me conform to male-dominated standards'. Such phrases were not current in Mary's day. She offered herself in unquestioning obedience. And the Christian message through the ages has always been a call to surrender to the divine will.

Yet the notion of obedience is now totally discredited in many fields of thought and action. A notion of worthwhile human behaviour has been cultivated which centres it, not in submission to demands, but in the casting off of external claims. I have said elsewhere (in *Where Do We Stand?*[1]) that the public has been fed for years on the myth of Escalating Emancipation, a basic fallacy which Christians need to tackle in the urgent task of demythologising secularism. It presents every step forward in the intellectual, the social, or the political field as a movement in a universal process of liberation from slavery. Labour is being 'freed' from slavery to capitalists, women from servitude to men, children from the tyranny of pedagogues, students from rigid academic disciplines, citizens from the constraints of poverty, women from the tyranny of ovulation, homosexuals from laws against perversion, couples from the prison of lifelong marriage, pregnant women from consequent labour.

The fact that some of these liberations were highly desirable has encouraged the notion that all of them must be so, indeed that 'progress' consists in getting rid of restrictions. We have already seen that theory to be based on a massive lie. It is based on the assumption that mankind has progressed, not by disciplining the unregenerate ego, but by giving it its fling. The theory is also based on the astounding proposition that the human race has been shackled throughout history, bogged down in a morass of inhibitions. The past which stretches out behind us is vaguely conceived as one of increasing blackness in the receding centuries. On the postulate of ever-spreading emancipation that must surely be the case. But if it is indeed so, then how on earth did people manage to build, to write, to paint, to compose, to sculpt the artistic masterpieces which these centuries of supposed darkness left behind? If individuality was so clogged and strangled in the days before Marx and Freud had pointed the way to social and personal fulfilment, how come the great cathedrals, the magnificent books, the breath-taking paintings — not to mention, from further back in the ages of pre-liberational paralysis, the discovery of the uses of fire, the invention of the wheel, of human language itself?

No one would wish to deny the great benefits which have been gained in the civilised world during the last 100 years in freeing men and women from servile toil, from economic exploitation, and from social injustice. But the myth of Escalating Emancipation assumes that there is no ceiling to such processes of amelioration, that the business of dismantling past restrictions can go on indefinitely. But it cannot. Even in the matter of freeing yourself from clothing there is a final stage. If you try to divest yourself further, then you will have to start tearing your hair out or ripping off your skin. There lies the fallacy in the myth of Escalating Emancipation. If we consider soberly what life will become like, were we to have a future of cumulative moral and social derestrictions comparable to those which have transformed life in the last few decades, we can only foresee a return to the jungle. We have had simulated acts of sodomy on the London stage. Further steps in extending permissiveness could but remove the element of simulation from the act and transfer it from the London stage to a London bus. There is a breaking-point which makes nonsense of the notion that human beings can go on casting off fetters, inhibitions, and restraints indefinitely. Sooner or later there will not be enough inhibitions to go round.

We have already observed the irony of the fact that great exponents of self-liberation end up in servitude to addictions. There is another irony in the fact that there are circumstances in which the great prophets of defying convention and regulation and acting creatively lay aside their principles. Observe a great prophet of self-liberation when he goes to an airport. Does he say, 'Watch me: no following the crowd for me: I'm going to do my own thing'? By no means. He lines up in the queue for tickets as meekly as you or I do. He files obediently through the security checks, responding accommodatingly to probes or questions. He follows directions given him like a lamb. He sits patiently in a row in the departure lounge, waiting submissively to be told what to do. There could surely be nothing today more like a Victorian school classroom than an airport departure lounge in which everybody waits to receive instructions from 'teacher'. 'Passengers with seats 1 to 20 proceed now to Gate A'. And the rebellious exponent of doing your own thing consults his ticket as meekly as you or I do, to see whether he is yet permitted to file out. What does the scene remind us of? 'Please teacher, may I be excused?' 'Yes, Johnny, you may go now. Be a good boy!'

Why do we all accept the outmoded disciplines of an authoritarian past when we travel by air? Because the safety of our own skins is at stake. This is not a case of possible damage to mind or soul. This is an area where physical well-being is at risk. So we put up with all the regulations the authorities choose to impose, knowing they ensure that we can travel in safety. It is nonsense to pretend that in the modern world regulation, discipline, and obedience to authority are outmoded. People who work in air-traffic control, or space-travel control, or a hospital operating theatre know well that regulation, discipline, and obedience are as essential as ever. You and I are relieved to know, when we put our precious bodies into the care of an airline, that no traffic controller is going to liberate himself from established code and rule when he is supposed to be talking down our plane. And we are relieved to know, too, when we put our precious bodies into the care of a hospital, that the surgeon can be trusted not to start defying code and formula, and instead to try doing his own thing creatively with the scalpel.

Massively organised human activities like air transportation or hospital surgery compulsively bring into play a seemingly outmoded machinery of rule and discipline and conformity, and do so in the interests of smooth functioning and effective fulfilment of their purposes. Must we assume that such activities are totally different from other joint ventures in which men and women co-operate for the general good? The effective operation of these systems is pervaded at every point by a demand for disciplined obedience. In other words, these systems, at every point at which they touch employees or passengers, healers or patients, insist on the total abandonment of those notions of what fruitful human activity consists in which our media and our educational systems project. The one thing that no one is allowed to do is his own thing. The one kind of conduct from which everyone is strictly required to abstain is breaking convention, not conforming, throwing off fetters, and asserting the individuality against the system.

The confrontation between the Church and the world is with us in all ages; but it would be false to imagine that there is some fundamental antithesis of principle between the ethic which determines the smooth functioning of our highly technologised civilisation and the discipline of the Christian life. On the contrary the antithesis lies between the ethic of discipline governing the life and determining the smooth functioning of our technological civilisation and the ethic of self-determination which is widely canvassed in our age. We have seen that civilisation could never have been built by the application of such an ethic, but that civilisation could be destroyed by it. To that extent Christianity and civilisation have common vested interests, just as the ethic of self-determination and jungle savagery have a common naked basis.

If we examine any of the great technological or bureaucratic mechanisms of modern life, air transport or electricity supply, health service or food supply, we see that only a complex network of interrelationships between part and part can guarantee the smooth functioning of the whole. The Christian Church is not a piece of machinery kept functioning by diverse operatives. Nor is it a welfare agency serviced by a bureaucracy. The biblical image of the Christian Church is that of a Body, a living body. It is in these terms that we are instructed to visualise the Christian community — a Body stretched out across the map of the world, and also stretched out across the map of history. The different parts of the Body, no less than the different parts of a machine, have to operate together in a complicated pattern of inter-dependence if the Body is to function healthily. The image of the Body of Christ into which all Christians are built in membership is central to Christian teaching. Membership of a common body is often cited in the very worthy cause of urging Christians to love one another, and to get together in mutual understanding across de-nominational frontiers. The call to unity and to mutual respect is one of the most logical implications to be de-rived from the doctrine of the Body. It is accepted that membership of the common Body requires us to be sen-sitive (within limits) to those of our contemporaries who, while sharing that membership, differ in interpre-tation of the Gospel message or of the kind of institu-tional fabric and discipline which ought to articulate the presence of the Body in the world. But there are equally logical implications of the doctrine of the Body which are too readily neglected or ignored. For instance, ought it not to be equally evident that relationship by member-ship of a common body requires us to be sensitive to those of our forebears who not only shared in that mem-bership but also by their witness, made possible ble the continuity of linkage which gives the Body its extension through time as well as through space?

You cannot amputate a finger or inject a serum into a flank without affecting the condition of the body as a whole. The Christian Body, spread out through the cen-turies, quivers in all its parts when some modern theologian takes his radical syringe and injects it with the serum of Arianism by an attack on the doctrine of the Incarnation, or when he takes his scalpel to scrape off the breast of its spiritual sensitivity by scepticism about the miraculous. Some liberal theologians are prepared to treat as expendable aspects of Christian truth which have circulated in the Body's bloodstream for centuries, giving it the corpuscular nourishment which guarantees its growth and survival. They clearly do not conceive of the Christian Church as a body living *through* history, increasing its strength by addition and enrichment. Indeed, they appear to regard it as a body in a state of such pampered invalidism that only if they perform the function of leeches and suck off quantities of its rich blood as superfluous can it survive.

Radical theology is obsessed with the passion for adjusting the faith to the changing fashions of the intellectual *Zeitgeist*. It is desperately anxious to be on good terms with 'the world'. Its fancy has been taken by the possibilities of reinvigorating the Christian Body with the supposed insights of humanistic secularism at a time when humanistic secularism is gasping on a bed of sickness. Since its condition is terminal, a great opportunity presents itself. Cut out the theological heart of the Christian Body. Transplant the heart from humanistic secularism in the hope of revitalising the Christian Body for a few more years. But every drop of healthy fluid in the Christian bloodstream rejects the donated organ.

Counter-Christianity

Liberal theologians today cast around for doctrines which they can write off as having been 'lived through', as though Christianity belonged to our age rather than to all time. They seem scarcely to treat seriously the Christian presupposition that the past is alive still in Jesus Christ our Lord. They launch novel propositions as though there were no such thing as accountability to history, to our forefathers in the faith, to those millions who taught and toiled and bled that we too in our own day might hear the Gospel of salvation.

Whenever an argument is conducted in a supposedly Christian context on the basis of presuppositions which Christianity itself would reject, then something we may call 'counter-Christianity' makes its appearance. Conduct an argument on the presupposition that Christian doctrine must be adjusted to accommodate itself to the twentieth-century anti-supernaturalist mind-set, and a basic truth about the status of Christianity is undermined. Counter-Christianity erodes the faith of believers by introducing secularist values and presuppositions into a professedly 'Christian' context. The characteristic of 'secularist values and judgements' is that they give pre-eminence to man-centred and world-centred (as opposed to God-centred) criteria, to limitedly temporal (as opposed to eternal) standpoints. Such judgements will not necessarily contain or imply a denial of God. Frank atheism will not corrupt Christians. Counter-Christianity contents itself with implying by its judgements that God is not the centre of things, that, though he exists, judgements need not be based on any prior recognition either of his existence or of his revealed word. In short, the starting-points of counter-Christian judgements are susceptible of being 'shared' by believers up to the point at which 'God' is involved.

Thus a journal records that an American Roman Catholic priest has declared that if Jesus wasn't a feminist, then he wasn't the Son of God. The writer of the article points out that the priest's first commitment is to the absolute of feminism. He is saying, 'If Jesus and Scripture do not agree with feminism, then there is something wrong with them'. This is a fairly extreme example of secularised thinking, but it is by no means unfamiliar in kind. Advocates of sexual libertinism have likewise asserted their belief that God cannot disapprove of behaviour which to them is desirable.

Man has always been tempted to form God in his own image, but a first postulate of Christianity is that man is made in God's image and is called to conduct himself accordingly. Whether Jesus was a feminist or whether God approves of sexual libertinism is in fact irrelevant to to the logical question whether such statements as the above will hold water. Christianity is a religion of revelation. God's will and purpose have been revealed to human beings through the events and prophecies of the Old Testament and through his personal intervention in human history in our Lord. The Church throughout her history, in so far as she has been true to the substance of this revelation, has continued to show forth that same divine will and purpose. Judgements about God can never take the form, 'He must be like this because that is what I feel he ought to be'. John Donne once remarked that you must have a very mean and unworthy estimate of God if you stipulate that he ought to behave as you yourself would behave if you were God.

Yet in the moral and theological spheres, we are today surrounded by mentors who would precisely thus reduce God's stature to the measure of their own. There was an old argument among philosophers whether a thing was good because God commanded it, or whether God commanded a thing because it was good. The layman is likely to be reminded of the dispute whether the hen precedes the egg or vice versa. But the argument suggests a healthier state of public logic than exists now. For here we have to take up the question whether a thing is good because God commands it, or whether it is good because man demands it.

This is not the place for a full-scale critique of theological liberalism. (The reader who seeks such a critique should turn to my book *A Defence of Dogmatism*.[2]) But it is appropriate here to point out how susceptible we are to arguments which speak to the heart rather than to the head. Appeals to the supposed finer feelings of men and women can easily masquerade as rational arguments. When it is postulated that a loving God must approve of this or that practice or attitude, because it is self-evident to us as twentieth-century human beings that nice, likeable people behave like that or think like that, then we need to check where our response may lead us.

Our only safeguard against being deceived is to draw a sharp line of demarcation between two modes of theological reasoning: that which has its roots in what God has revealed to man, and that which has its roots in what man fabricates, whether to suit his personal predilections or the fashion of the age. Christians today who find their faith assaulted by theological attacks on traditional teaching need to have this crucial line of demarcation clarified. It is easy to cross the line by specious argument. Perhaps the argument makes a superficial appeal to compassion: 'A loving God could never disapprove of people giving full physical expression to a relationship so deep.' Or perhaps the argument is aimed at the man-in-the-street's common sense: 'You surely can't believe in a God who does conjuring tricks with the contents of a boy's shopping-basket.' The argument is received sympathetically, and a Rubicon has been crossed, separating faith in a revealed God from the manufacture of a deity to accommodate human taste.

Thus in the ethical field we find supposedly 'Christian' voices discrediting the notion that fornication and adultery should be described as 'sins'. They certainly do not recommend this shift in moral thinking by an appeal to Scripture and tradition. They do not even claim that modern critical scholarship is now in a position to set the record straight; they do not explain that only the clumsiness of translators and the intrusive emendations of editors have obscured the actual dominical teaching, and that what our Lord said to the woman taken in adultery was not after all 'Go and sin no more' but 'Keep it up, and good luck to you'. No, they take their stand on nothing so solid as such advanced critical scholarship. They take their stand on the philosophy of the human being as a jack-in-the-box lidded down for centuries by mechanical inhibitions in the blackness of constraint. Unclasp the lid, hinge it open, and the child of God bounces up into the freedom of the daylight. Prohibitions are no more. Anything is good if it is 'creative', 'self-fulfilling', 'self-liberating', 'life-enhancing', 'self-enriching', 'self-realising', 'integrative', and so on. There are few sexual acts known to the human race which cannot be approved by the criteria.

There should be no surprise that these bogus values should be rustled up by atheistic and humanistic psychologists. What is surprising is that they are sometimes taken up by supposedly 'Christian' counsellors. And the development is the more ironic in that there are Christians working professionally in the field of psychology who are doing their best to clear the air of delusive concepts. Paul Vitz, a Professor of Psychology at New York University, has made a bold critique of modern psychology in his book *Psychology as Religion: The Cult of Self-Worship*.[3] He analyses current humanistic theories which revolve around what is virtually worship of the self. He finds it easy to display the irrelevance of current ideals of independence, self-actualisation, and creative activity to human beings who are face to face with suffering or frustration, disease or death. And he is critical of 'liberal churches' which 'have often enthusiastically embraced selfism and humanistic psychology without regard to its hostility to Christian teaching'.

It is interesting to find a Professor of Psychology arguing that selfist psychology which caters for what has been called the 'Me generation' is no fit prescription for human beings in a life which includes suffering and failure, for a prime argument of this book is that doctrinal dilution of Christian teaching is no fit prescription for human beings who face the emergencies of mortality. Though psychology has not perhaps in Western Europe achieved the pseudo-religious status that it has achieved in the United States, there is no doubt that the distinctions Vitz makes between Christian presuppositions and secularist presuppositions in the psychological field need to be brought home to those within the Church who too readily latch on to the vocabulary of 'selfist' psychology.

We Christians need to examine what reaches us in the way of psychological advice or instruction from counsellors or writers, whether professional or amateur. We must be on the watch against erroneous teaching. A good idea might be to formulate a series of questions which will serve as touchstones in this respect:

— Does this advice or teaching recognise that God is our Father and Creator to whom we owe obedience, or does it presuppose that the individual is an autonomous being subject to no such authority?

— Does this advice or teaching recognise that the human being has an eternal destiny and derives his or her personal significance and value from God himself, or does it presuppose that the individual has an earthly life only and can define his or her full worth at the limitedly human level?

— Does this advice or teaching recognise a code of morality based on absolute values, or does it presuppose that all morality is relative and that in self-expression we can find our own moral moorings?

— Does this advice or teaching allow that love of God and of others will demand self-conquest and self-sacrifice, or does it give primacy to ideals of self-realisation in personal development?

— Does this advice or teaching allow for the need for penitence, forgiveness, and restitution to others, or does it tend to play down any sense of guilt and to explain all difficulties in terms of external causes?

It is only on the basis of some such strict application of Christian criteria that we can prevent ourselves from being brainwashed by the exponents of what Paul Vitz calls 'selfism', theorists for whom the individual is the 'sole centre of legitimate moral choice'.

Development of Permissiveness

We have grown accustomed to talk of the 'sexual revolution' of the last two or three decades. It is notable, however, that when 'theologians' first jumped on this bandwagon by publicly advertising 'permissiveness' in the 1960s, they did not immediately argue on the basis of the jack-in-the-box theory. They found it necessary to cite instances in which 'breaking the commandments' by, say, adultery or fornication was seemingly justified by some unselfish motive of satisfying the desires of some perhaps emotionally frustrated partner. Advocates of situational ethics projected situations, real or fictional, in which conscientious men and women heroically broke the Christian moral code by lovingly taking frustrated partners to bed and making them happy. There was one fictional situation from film-land telling of a repressed, unfulfilled, self-distrustful young sailor who goes with a prostitute but is too nervous to take the initiative. The prostitute, seeing his desperate psychological need, satisfies his sexual hunger in such a way that he is left self-confident and grown up at last. 'He goes away a deeper and fuller person than he came in. What is seen is an act of charity which proclaims the glory of God.'[4] Although C S Lewis, for one, early pointed out that the theme of the 'honest whore' (where 'honest' meant 'chaste') was as old as the hills in literature, a great to-do was created by the supposed revolutionary discoveries of the 'new moralists' in positing a contradiction between 'Christian charity' which is concerned about nothing so much as 'making others happy' and a Christian moral code which denies honest men and women the right to make use of their sexual proclivities extramaritally for this very purpose.

Whatever may be said of the logic of those who invented novelettes to press the alternative ethic of counter-Christianity, at least they did *pretend* to recommend permissive behaviour on the grounds of benefit to others. This meant that sincere Christians could be taken in by their arguments. The notion that God is love and the specious corollary that any act which gives immediate satisfaction to another person at any given moment must therefore have God's blessing are not perhaps easily distinguishable by simple minds. This specious theory did its work, of course, by blinkering the mind to all crucial first principles of Christian morality — the Word of God, the will of God, and the overriding demand to give them precedence over the apparent claims of immediate earthly and physical 'well-being'. Nevertheless, the appeal to altruism, though superficial, was enough to soften up the Christian conscience to acceptance of so-called 'permissiveness'. And the next step in the formulation of the alternative ethic, a powerful instrument of counter-Christianity, was to eliminate the need even for an altruistic motive for self-indulgence. The new 'duty' became, not making others happy, but making yourself happy. A theory of personality borrowed from atheistic psychology (and always heavily under fire from genuine Christian psychologists) began to be propounded in the name of Christianity. Briefly, its emphasis was on 'self-actualisation' or 'self-realisation'. An act is good according to this code in so far as it contributes to the development of the personality. It is everyone's responsibility to maximise his own human potential, to turn himself into a complete, mature, integrated person. The total absence of reference to objective standards here is symptomatic of a code utterly subjective and relative in its evaluations.

This code is now a keystone of the alternative ethic and therefore of counter-Christianity. Yet you will easily find echoes from it in sermons and diocesan leaflets, in religious journals and publications. And what it basically amounts to is that virtue resides in making yourself feel good. Feelings are as crucial to the alternative code as they are peripheral to genuine Christian morality. For notions of exploring your full potential, of realising the complete you, of experiencing yourself as an integrated whole, all lay stress on what the individual feels like, and all studiously avoid reference to virtues or vices, or, indeed, to any obligations to others or to God. It is astonishing that Christans should have allowed their thinking to be infected by a 'moral code' which not only allows of no reference to God, but positively substitutes for duty to God and duty to your neighbour the isolated duty to yourself. It is no exaggeration to say that we have here an ethic — in various forms often appealed to in supposedly 'Christian' contexts — which replaces love of God and love of your neighbour by self-love. In short, the alternative ethic turns Christian morality upside down. It is frankly rooted in the principle of self-gratification. When the early exponents of situational ethics began the first assault on the fortress of traditional Christian morality, they perhaps little guessed what would happen after they had knocked a hole in the wall. Urging the bending of objective standards and moral rules in subservience to the demands of so-called 'love' and 'compassion' prepared the way, by discrediting standards and rules, for the obliteration of all ethical guidelines and their replacement by the banner of anarchic self-gratification.

Anyone with the least knowledge of history and the least susceptibility to the influence of the past upon the present must be astounded by the confidence of the advocates of the alternative ethic in implying that human nature has been totally misunderstood by the civilised West until the last 50 years or so, and that the weight of a 2,000 year consensus of judgement in respect of personal morality counts as nothing beside the insights of post-Freudian psychology.

Wherever 'new' thinking relies for its validity on the assumption that on crucial moral issues the best wisdom of law-makers and the common sense of the man in the street have been for centuries dead wrong, the onus of proof lies firmly on the innovators. That is not to say that the innovators will always be proved wrong. If that were the case, then slavery would be with us still, and child labour in mines and factories. But it should be noticed that the progressivists who made the first moves to get rid of such abuses had no need to bring into question the word of God in the Scriptures. On the contrary, they appealed to that Word, and on the strength of that appeal touched the consciences of fellow Christians. The permissiveness of the alternative ethic, on the other hand, as it intrudes into Christendom, presupposes that St Paul did not know what he was talking about. It assumes that the progress of knowledge since his time is such that he and his fellows are unreliable guides to human conduct in such subtle matters as sexual behaviour. But there is no evidence that succeeding ages have advanced in understanding either of the nature of man or of the kind of moral behaviour that is appropriate to him. Indeed, succeeding generations have for centuries persisted in turning back to the Bible precisely for guidance about human conduct.

In this respect, two features of the contemporary scene stand in stark contrast, indeed, in mutual contradiction.

The first is the popular conviction that now at last, after centuries of ignorance, we really understand the human personality and its needs: the second is that our civilisation is marked by an epidemic of mental disease and mental disturbance apparently unparalleled in history. Cynics have suggested that the incidence of mental disorders increases in direct ratio to the increase in psychological studies and psycho-therapeutic practice. No one would wish to belittle the achievements of a science whose practitioners, as each of us can recall, have restored to health and well-being the victims of grave depression and graver aberrations still. But it is the overall judgement upon our age that is here at issue, and in particular whether its record gives it the right to sit in judgement upon other ages in respect of this particular matter — understanding of the human personality and, more especially, of what kind of behaviour by individuals contributes to their own mental stability, to the stability of their kin and friends, and to the harmonious functioning of the society to which they belong. And in relation to this general question, packed mental hospitals, individual collapses, family breakdowns, and social tensions, not to mention juvenile delinquency, teenage violence, drug addiction, and adult vandalism stare us in the face, assuring us that, whatever else we may claim to be masters of in twentieth-century Western Europe, understanding of the secret of ordered harmonious personal life is not our strong point.

The argument that 'we know better nowadays' is sometimes used with hilarious inappropriateness. I have read a solemn, seemingly scholarly, formulation of this case in relation to the biblical condemnation of adultery and sodomy. It was explained that understanding of human nature was comparatively primitive even

in New Testament times; that St Paul and his like lacked
our subtle awareness of the complex, indeed, highly varied make-up of the human creature as a sexual being and
of the consequently multifarious needs of his awakened
sensitivities. Such needs could never be catered for by
blanket formulations crudely banning extramarital sex
or homosexual practices in all circumstances. The
teachers of the past whose precepts have nourished millions of Christians and given stability to their lives made
the mistake of thinking that they knew what was good
and what was evil.

That is an interesting argument, but what follows it is
positively astounding. The claim is made that today,
after massive advances in physiological and psychological scholarship, we now realise that the codification of
sexual mores by our early teachers was based on a
simplification quite inappropriate to the complexity of
the human realities, and on a habit of generalisation
quite inappropriate to the immense variation of those
human realities. So what does the conclusion of the
latest scholarship amount to? It amounts to this: We now
know that it is far too early in human history to define
exactly what is proper and what is improper in human
conduct in the heterosexual and homosexual fields. It is
too early therefore to promulgate general rules about
what is good and what is evil. It is too early in the
advance of civilisation to tell our Christian congrega-
tions that this or that is sinful. In other words, we now
know that we do not know. Thanks to the massive
explorations in psychological study, the human race has
at last advanced from supposed knowledge to accepted
ignorance.

God is a God of Love and Justice, and if therefore he
asks a certain kind of behaviour of men and women, we

can be sure that he will not make it impossible for them to discern what that behaviour is. There has never been any doubt that the God revealed in Jesus Christ asked certain things of them in the way of moral behaviour. Christ himself, even by unbelievers, is recognised as a great moral teacher. A God who comes to earth to make himself known will not, if he loves mankind and cares about how they behave, make it impossible for them to know what is good and what is evil. Nor will he, if he loves his human family, leave loose ends to be cleared up over a matter so central, so crucial and pervasive in the personal careers of men and women, as their sexuality. There is not a single passage in the New Testament, not a sentence, not a hint to suggest that such issues as sexual conduct need further exploration before pronouncement can be made on what is permissible and what is sinful. What kind of God do we turn the God of Love into if he is not capable even of making clear whether a man ought to go to bed with another man's wife? What kind of God do we turn the God of Truth into if he is capable through his word, his prophets, his saints and teachers for 2,000 years of utterly misleading his children over the propriety of homosexual practices? What kind of God do we turn the God of Justice into if he waits 20 centuries before hinting to his children that after all what was really meant by the 10 Commandments and the Sermon on the Mount was that everyone must realise his own individual potential in whatever ways he finds most fully expressive of his own feelings?

Atheistic humanists who preach the secularist gospels of naturalistic well-being and hedonistic self-gratification can perhaps claim consistency for their position. But those who pretend to stand in the Christian tradition as theologians and teachers, as priests and counsellors, and who preach the same gospels under a 'Christian' label, can make no such claim. Whether in the sphere of doctrine or morality, theologians who try to turn the tables on what has been learned by revelation of God and his ways automatically ally themselves with 'the world'. Self-gratification as a key principle of morality is the matching heresy to self-determination as a key principle of theology. We decide what is right for us to do by an appeal to our feelings, and we decide what is right for us to believe by an appeal to our preferences. It ought not to be necessary for anyone to have to observe that these are not Christian options.

The fact that it *is* necessary arises because we have among our clergy and teachers, theologians and bishops, people who live in a permanent coma in respect of history, who are paralysed in mind and nerve in respect of that vibrancy from the past which still shudders through our living institutions. We have among us clergy and teachers nourished on the sub-theology that rejects history in favour of immediacy, that has reduced supernatural faith to a matter of personal boost, and transcendental truth to something to be arrived at by counting votes. Professing Christians for whom the Holy Spirit is the official who rubber-stamps the decisions of a sadly untutored synod and the avuncular friend who treats you to nods and winks in favour of doing your own thing can never turn the tide of secularism, for they are themselves ambassadors of secularism within the Church of God. Clergy who have been long addicted to the needle of modernity will need a severely disciplined course of treatment if they are to recover. The secularist pushers must be kept at bay and the withdrawal agonies tempered by a rigorous regimen. The necessary remedies are to hand in the medications of self-examination, contrition, and penance. The lead ought surely to be taken by those fathers-in-God who have publicly tried to subvert the faith of those souls entrusted to their charge.

There is an expression used in medicine — 'introgenic disease' — to describe a disorder produced by a doctor, usually as a result of medication given for another disease. Many of the ills of the Church today are 'introgenic', produced by misguided would-be healers of ailments which are sometimes imaginary and, where they are genuine, are generally less damaging than the introgenic disorders produced by the treatment itself. Permissiveness became the vogue with trendy clergymen when the early advocates of the 'new morality' with their 'situational ethics' tried to remedy the supposed weaknesses of formulated rules. They behaved as though they were the first people to discover that the codification of rules for moral conduct produces generalisations which can be shown not to hold water in certain hypothetical human dilemmas. But it has always been accepted that moral and legal generalisations are rough and ready. Proverbial wisdom insists that 'the exception proves the rule'. The poor woman who steals bread for a starving child is not a new concept. The presentation of formulated rules, legal and moral, has always presupposed a degree of common sense in the public to whom they were addressed.

The 'new morality' of the 1960s was bred of an attempt to heal Christendom of slavish attachment to formulas and literal interpretation of general rules at a time when Christendom was suffering from no such zeal in unintelligent conscientiousness but from sheer apathy. Devotees of theological radical chic exercised their ingenuity in seeking instances of heroic 'Christian love' which refused to be fettered by crude moral laws against fornication and adultery. Twenty years or so later it is painfully clear how misapplied their ingenuity was. By and large, men and women were not defying their Creator by locking up his gift of sexuality in a box and refusing to share it with others because it was against the rules. There was no plethora of smugly chaste Christians rejoicing in their invulnerability while hungry potential partners of the opposite sex, or of the same sex, prowled about in the torment of neurosis through lack of their sexual attentions. There has been no prudish cultivation of chastity, no priggish immersion in virginal self-protectiveness to create psychological havoc among our contemporaries. The theological 'new morality' of the 1960s was as defective in its diagnosis as it was disastrous in its recommendations.

The Decomposition of Public Morality

It has long been out of fashion to refer to such virtues as chastity, fidelity, or temperance in public discussion of personal difficulties to which, in Christian terms, they are crucially relevant. In their place, speakers and writers have recourse to the selfish pseudo-values of the alternative ethic such as 'self-awareness' and the like. They also misuse a nebulous vocabulary of approval-noises and disapproval-noises for the purpose of what can only be called brainwashing the public. Thus we saw how H A Williams' young man came away from his experience with the prostitute a 'deeper fuller person than he came in'. He has now got 'confidence' and 'self-respect'. And Williams followed this example with the story of a man attracted to young girls who takes a woman of his own age away for a weekend. Only sleeping with her will give him the 'confidence' he needs to escape his abnormality. 'Will he be able to summon up the necessary courage or not?' Well, he does, and he is healed, 'made whole'. 'And the appropriate response is — Glory to God in the Highest'.[5] Thus words like 'courage', 'self-respect', 'whole', 'deeper' and 'fuller', are used as pure approval-noises, having no strict logical connection with the situations described. On this basis, the converse disapproval-noises can be dragged in to make chaste or unselfish behaviour appear cowardly, shallow, or empty.

The pseudo-vocabulary of the alternative ethic has over the years acquired a life of its own. In sexual relationships people are urged to be honest, true to themselves, self-giving, positive, mature, adult, generous, life-affirming, unafraid, open, and so on. Any word will do, however irrelevant, if it can touch the feelings as an approval-noise. Any word will do so long as the concepts of chastity, fidelity, and temperance are veiled from view.

The moral brainwashing of the public at large has been made possible because there is an influential school of thought which judges the handing on of rigid moral advice to be an interference in personal liberty. The individual's freedom of choice is paramount, and it is a freedom of choice based on inner impulse. It is not proper for any formal rule to stand in the way of what gratifies the individual. In this connection, an interesting suggestion has recently been made in *The Times* by John Rae, formerly headmaster of Westminster School and now Director of the Laura Ashley Foundation. He rightly traces back the ultimate origin of contemporary permissiveness to the Bloomsbury Group of Edwardian days. This is true in the sense that the 1960s made available to everybody a way of life earlier adopted by a sophisticated cultural élite. Rae stresses especially the 'elevation of self' and 'the emphasis on immediate gratification'. He then draws a remarkable parallel between the lack of sexual restraint and the rejection of thrift. He argues that 'self-indulgent behaviour and easy credit' are 'two aspects of the same permissive value system'. He sees a common denominator of sexual and acquisitive permissiveness in the message, 'If you want it, have it now; there is no longer any virtue in thrift or self-restraint'.[6]

This is an illuminating parallel. A remarkable feature of our civilisation is that as we dispense with disciplines in some fields, we impose them in others. Whether you kill an unborn child, or whether you purchase £3,000 worth of goods you cannot afford to pay for, is a matter of free choice — but not whether you strap yourself into the front seat of your car with a seat-belt. If physical safety is at issue, the weight of the law increasingly comes down in support of it. If moral or spiritual well-being is at issue, even the tacit codes of our civilised past are scrapped in favour of slogans such as 'Be yourself' or 'Do your own thing'.

Outside the Christian world this is understandable. The great liberation-model of modern secularism is the man or woman who one day decides to break with the conventions of married life, of monogamy, of the nuclear family, or of heterosexuality, to become himself or herself. 'I must discover myself anew. My real self has been overlaid by futile attempts to stereotype myself as husband or wife, as bread-winner or home-maker. I have tried to adjust to the bogus norms of outmoded codes.' And off he or she goes to frolic with the gays or the lesbians. But the great liberation-model of modern Christianity is far different. It is represented by people like Mother Teresa of Calcutta. She too breaks with the conventional life-style of marriage and the home — but not in order to find herself, rather in order to lose herself. So she described to Malcolm Muggeridge how she embarked on her work. 'I was so sure then, and I'm still convinced that it was he and not I.' 'I wanted to serve the poor purely for the love of God.' And what is her advice to seekers after spiritual progress? 'Make sure that you let God's grace work in your souls by accepting whatever he gives you, and giving him whatever he takes of you.'

There is a diabolical conspiracy at work in the Western world. Its aim is to decompose the fabric of morality and civilisation. We know that it is diabolical from the fact that its first postulate is that obedience to God's law is nonsense. You must make your own mind up. You must do whatever your desires and whims dictate. All emphasis is ostensibly laid on individual choice and responsibility, while, in fact, true choice and responsibility are often lifted from the shoulders of those who make a mess of things. Consider the way in which we now talk of marriage as something which two people possess and share but which may turn sour like some foodstuff that is kept too long. 'Their marriage has irretrievably broken down', we say as though the thing were a car which had finally cracked up. There it stands at the roadside, its cylinders seized up and its transmission done for. The only thing to do is to have the useless object towed away into the scrap yard. Or we say, 'They're having trouble with their marriage: it isn't working as it should' or, 'They're desperately trying to do something about their marriage: I don't think they'll be able to salvage it'. At one moment marriage is likened to a central heating system that has let them down; at the next moment it sounds like a damaged motor launch out of which the parties are feverishly bailing water in an effort to keep it afloat.

Is there any such thing as 'a marriage' which can go right or wrong? There are two people who have made certain vows and can either keep them or break them. There are two human beings who can live in harmony, who can fight like cat and dog or who can live in quiet indifference. But if they choose to quarrel, is there in any sense a THING that has broken down? Of course there is not. Strictly speaking, 'marriage' itself cannot fail anyone. Men and women can fail to live up to it as they can fail in dozens of other ways. But the failure is *their* failure. It is no more logical to say, 'I'm having trouble with my marriage: it isn't working as it should' than it would be to say, 'I'm having trouble with my baptism: it isn't working as it should. I may have to swap it for another model'. Of course, in marital disputes one partner may be by far the greater offender. The other partner may be totally or almost totally innocent. Moreover, disaster may strike, and husband or wife may find themselves with a partner afflicted with multiple sclerosis, with alcoholism, or with a gravely abnormal mental condition. The circumstances may be such that only a heroic saint could fulfil the vow of continuing support, love, and fidelity. None of us, especially if we are happily married, has the right to pass judgement on men and women who have faced agonising dilemmas of this kind. Nevertheless, even in the extreme case, logic requires us to insist that what fails is not 'a marriage' but human beings, perhaps a human being no longer responsible for his or her actions, perhaps a human being tested beyond endurance.

The effect of pretending that there is this rather unmanageable thing, a 'marriage', is to allow us to picture two innocent people feverishly trying to do something to

protect and preserve a common possession that is getting out of hand — something perhaps like a pet dog
which has turned unruly and started to bite visitors. In
this way we mentally shift responsibility from the shoulders of free human beings. Both parties are enabled to
wring their hands over a misfortune which has descended
upon them through no fault of their own. The marriage
seemed to be a good buy. Great care has been lavished on
it. Yet it has let its owners down. Thus, in this little
example of the way we talk of marriage, while the
rhetoric of secular permissiveness is all about being
yourself, making your own choices, and doing your own
thing, the actual practical application of permissiveness
is to shift reponsibility from human beings, not on to
other human beings, but on to an imaginary thing, a
'marriage' or a 'relationship'. There is an abdication of
human freedom and responsibility grotesque in its
thoroughness. And this instance we have given — of the
way we use words in a particular series of expressions
on the subject of marriage — provides a clear example of
the way our thinking is secularised stage by stage. Shift-
ing personal responsibility from men and women is a
crucial process in thoroughly de-Christianising our
society. With all the talk of 'choice', men and women are
virtually deprived of choice and made the victims of
chance. Lucky men and women stumble into a happy,
durable marriage, while unlucky ones come away from
the same market with a model which at first sight looks
just as good, but turns out on closer acquaintance to be a
dud model which would not last even the noblest pair a
twelvemonth.

This kind of thinking is but fruit on the growth of that
naturalistic tree which Eve bowed down to worship in
her newly fallen state. In other words, the scarcely

conscious abandonment of freedom evidenced in the way couples treat and talk of their 'marriage' springs logically from the basic decision to worship the 'strong brown god' instead of taming him, to make of the natural order, whence our appetites derive and in which our emotional life is rooted through the senses themselves, the only source of meaning and value. The 'authority' with which modernity has endowed the transient feelings and whims of men and women in connection with their human relationships, and even with their ephemeral aesthetic perceptions, represents a key idolatry which any serious attempt to demythologise secularism must tackle head on. Fundamentally, it is an idolatry of the untranscended natural order, of the 'brown god' and the rifled tree.

Because, as we have seen, the true status of the natural order is such that it must be tamed and disciplined, an age which recognises no authority or source of meaning superior to the natural order will lapse into slavery to it. The material works of civilisation cannot be constructed except by the taming alike of the river to be bridged and of the human brains and human hands which devise and construct the required machinery. The institutional frameworks of civilisation are the products of the same process. It follows that secularism, by recognising no authority in deference to which the 'strong brown god' can be tamed and the lure of the deadly tree resisted, is philosophically speaking irreconcilable with civilisation. This is the logic of the case we have made. It explains why all around us we see evidence of civilised structures, material and institutional, under threat of decomposition. We have seen, too, how in the environment of the natural order the human being who defers to no authority superior to it and recognises no authority superior to it inevitably becomes its slave. It follows that secularism is irreconcilable with true freedom. And this explains why all around us we see evidence of human beings, physically and mentally, under threat of decomposition by addiction to the fruits of the poisoned tree.

Decomposition is eating away the fabric of civilisation, material, cultural, and human. Anyone who thinks that the destruction of the environment by acid rain or nuclear fall-out is unrelated to the destruction of the family by divorce and promiscuity is living in a dream world. Anyone who thinks that vandalism, mounting crime, and unsafe city streets are unrelated to the corruption of the child mind by teachers brought up on the educational doctrines of naturalistic free expression is living in a dream world. Anyone who thinks that piling up armaments of destruction without and destroying the body within by heroin or by homosexual practices are unrelated phenomena is closing his eyes to the truth. Perhaps nothing could be more revealing of the deep connection between evils besetting us than the discovery of medical men who are investigating the condition of the victims of Chernobyl. They have found a similarity between the breakdown of the immunity system in victims of that disaster and in AIDS victims.

We have recently observed the absurdity of people arguing whether AIDS is a divinely devised punishment for the sin of sodomy. Since women and children, as well as male users of the syringe and haemophiliacs, all alike innocent of homosexual practices, have become victims of the scourge, it is ridiculous to think in terms of a system of divine tit for tat. But to imagine therefore that you can insulate a phenomenon like AIDS from the sphere of human affairs over which divine providence and divine judgement operate would be absurd. The natural order has been devised in such a way that certain consequences follow from certain human actions. If you go out in a thunderstorm, you may get struck by lightning whether you are a wicked old reprobate or an innocent child. If you pluck an attractive looking berry from a poisoned bush and eat it, you will die whether you are a debilitated debauchee or a healthy little infant. The natural order is alive with 'traps' dangerous alike to the foolish, the wilful, the unwary, and the innocent. We accept such matters, most of us, without bringing God to book. There are other calamities in life where an element of culpable human wilfulness, carelessness, or callousness intrudes more directly, such as a road accident caused by bad driving or a plane crash caused by careless maintenance. Lastly, there are calamities whose cause is totally and directly the consequence of human wickedness, like the horrors of Auschwitz. For the person concerned to think logically, the question of God's good providence is least likely to arise where the suffering of the innocent is plainly the result of human malevolence. For the logically-minded, the question of God's good providence is surely much more likely to arise when an innocent child is killed by lightning than when 10,000 men and women are gassed by their captors in a concentration camp. Numbers quite naturally tend to overwhelm us with horror, but death is total for one human being in isolation however many human beings are killed. Ten people with toothache is not more painful for anyone than one person with toothache. The mystery of suffering, the problem of pain, the question it raises of God's providence, is as sharp when one innocent child is killed by lightning as it is when 100,000 people die of starvation.

The multiplication table cannot complicate for

Christians the mystery of God's providence. Anyone who is in this particular respect more teased intellectually by the phenomenon of Hiroshima than by that of the two-year-old next door who walks into a foot-deep garden pond and falls face down in it never to get up again is simply not a logical thinker and quite unfitted for philosophical speculation. The natural order is so devised that people can drown themselves in pools, that people can kill themselves by drinking too much alcohol, that people can get and convey venereal diseases by sexual promiscuity, and can acquire and spread AIDS by homosexual practices especially. It would be absurd to pretend that human culpability is of the same kind and is present to the same degree in the spreading of AIDS, the slaughter on the roads, the bombing of Hiroshima, and the holocaust of Auschwitz. But it would be even more absurd to deny that all these evils are the product of human sin, the consequence of human depravity. All are aspects of what happens in a divinely created universe when men and women are disobedient. The fact that the innocent suffer alongside the guilty troubles the mind. But a world in which only the guilty suffered would be a world deprived of freedom.

I have just listened to a bishop on the radio pussyfooting charitably around the subject of AIDS and leaning over backwards not to sound judgemental about homosexuality. One sympathises with anyone called upon to comment publicly on this tragic subject. AIDS is a positively terrifying scourge. Few of us could trust ourselves to do other than mumble clichés about compassion if faced with the need to say something to an audience about an enormity so numbingly bleak. Any condemnation of homosexual practices would seem now like a brutal attack on a community already suffering to a degree which must call out sympathy from any humane person. It would look like kicking a man who is flat on his back already. The principle that the deepest compassion for the sinner can coexist with the sharpest condemnation of the sin is, of course, crucial to Christian practice. There is small need to underline the fact that the spread of AIDS in the West has been primarily the consequence of homosexual libertarianism. If an alcoholic is dying of cirrhosis of the liver or *delirium tremens*, we do not keep reminding him that he is paying the price of his addiction. If a heavy smoker is dying of cancer of the lung, we do not keep reminding him that he is paying the price of his addiction.

The spread of AIDS certainly seem to mark the end of a phase. The 'sexual revolution' which legitimised homosexual practices and encouraged heterosexual promiscuity was essentially based on two principles. The first was that people should be able to act as they chose in private, provided that their acts did not damage other people. The second was the right of individuals, with various sexual inclinations, to 'self-fulfilment' or self-gratification, a key principle of what we have called the happiness-orientated ethic. But it is clear now that, in the first place, indulging in homosexual practices and heterosexual promiscuity can no longer be said to do no grave damage to others. Infected haemophiliacs, infected wives, and babies infected at birth are evidence of that. It is also clear, in the second place, that a sexual libertarianism once demanded and justified by reference to a happiness-orientated ethic can no longer be validly defended when it proves in fact to engender human misery and suffering on a terrifyingly massive scale. In short, the initial justifications for the 'sexual revolution' of the 1960s have been totally undermined.

AIDS will surely kill the lie that sexual morality is a wholly private matter. A key principle of the alternative ethic, that what individuals do in private is their own affair, is now null and void. The attitude is exploded which would put 'private morality' in sexual matters exactly on a par with individual political opinions which everybody has the right to keep to himself, even an applicant for a job involving close and intimate contact with the young. We have already seen in our analysis of such crimes as assault and theft that evil deeds are not isolated individual acts. They are part of a network of evil extended through human history. Evil is essentially infectious. Human affairs are so managed and human relationships so conducted that, quite apart from the damage done to immediate contacts by the spread of sexual sins, there is a corruption of the public atmosphere, a soiling of the public mind which can touch us all.

A telling incident occurred recently which drives the point home for me. The ducks on Derwentwater seem to have been thoroughly corrupted by tourists. Approach the lake-side with a paper bag which looks as though it might possibly contain currant buns or potato crisps, and the sharp-eyed ducks will quickly forsake the tedious task of foraging under water for whatever living or dead matter supplies them with their natural sustenance in favour of the easier option of feeding on morsels thrown to them by soft-hearted visitors. It so happened that we had to dispose of a packet of uneaten sandwiches rapidly going stale, and they were put into my hand when I took an afternoon walk one day. Sure enough I was soon surrounded by ducks as I broke the bread in pieces and tried to distribute them as fairly as I could.

Within a few minutes, I was joined by a charming little

girl of about three. Naturally I began to give her pieces of bread to hand on to the ducks. But it was not long before she was called back abruptly by observant parents. They were plainly, and quite understandably, alarmed that she should so easily make friends with a strange man. That is the world we now live in. And for its infected mental climate we are indebted to three decades of campaigning for permissiveness in which the theological 'new moralists' of the 1960s played their part. If you want to measure how far the supposedly private sins of individuals infect the public mental climate of the day, reflect what would happen if Jesus Christ sat on the lakeside of Derwentwater or of the Serpentine in 1987 and said, 'Suffer the little children to come unto me'. Honest, God-fearing parents would have to call their little ones away from him, reminding them sternly never, *never* to speak to a strange man, but always, *always* to run away from him.

Signs of Hope

At the end of a chapter concerned to highlight some of the more dismal aspects of the mental climate in which we live today, it is right to note new signs of hope. One of the most heartening developments in Christendom during the last decade has been the growth of co-operation, in the USA especially, between Christians of different denominations who, by digging deep, mentally and spiritually, at the centre of their respective denominations, have found that they are at one in their resistance to the disease of creeping secularisation infecting all denominations. Its symptoms are a questioning of revealed truth, a sapping of confidence in all vehicles of spiritual nourishment, whether biblical or institutional, and a deflection of energy and focus from questions of conversion and salvation to questions of earthly welfare. But God brings good out of evil. Resistance to the inter-denominational disease has resulted in healthy new trans-denominational alliances. Roman Catholics, who are 'evangelical' in their passion for personal rootedness in Christ and for adherence to the Scriptures, have allied themselves with Protestant evangelicals, who are 'catholic' in their awareness of the need for intellectual comprehensiveness. Together they face the threat of secularist pressures within the churches to reduce Christianity to the status of a merely supportive religion, a religion devoted not to undermining worldliness but to cosseting it.

In 1980 a group of Roman Catholic and Protestant evangelical scholars and pastoral leaders met at Ann Arbor, Michigan, for the first of a series of conferences on the challenge facing Christians from what I have called 'counter-Christianity'. Their papers and contributions were collected and published under the title *Christianity Confronts Modernity*.[7] The book includes a telling contribution by James Hitchcock, 'The Course of Radical Change in the Churches'. No clearer or more concise account of the attitudes which characterise counter-Christianity could be found than is contained in this contribution. Hitchcock points to the futility of trying to accommodate Christian beliefs to the ephemeral 'spirit of the age' and the danger of sacrificing authoritative Christian truth to the specious 'demands of modernity'. He shows how Christian love degenerates into sentimentality, while energy is expended in preventing the Church from taking firm moral stands. Our notion of freedom is secularised by 'worldly notions of personal rights'. Individual desires are allotted a bogus pre-eminence; the

notion of self-denial is superseded by that of self-fulfilment. Christians unknowingly imbibe a secularist way
of looking at the world and then make that their standard
of measurement.

Diagnoses of this kind are indeed meat and drink to
those hungry and thirsty for a clear Christian lead
through the jungle of contemporary relativism. They are
surely a sign of a new awakening. Writers are perhaps
over-fond of locating turning-points in history.
Nevertheless, there is a good deal of evidence to suggest
that we have latterly reached a historical turning-point.
A literary historian who has spent many years working
in the field of recent literature naturally acquires a
heightened sensitivity to movements of the mind
through the successive decades of our age. When I was
recently asked to revise and update for a new edition my
book *Twentieth-Century English Literature* (Macmillan
History of Literature), which I had written in the late
1970s, the task faced me of having to sum up relevant
developments in the 6 years or so since the original text
was completed. I found myself having to refer to crucial
changes of attitude brought by the 1980s, including of
course the 'rolling back of the tide of sexual permissiveness released in the 1960s'. There have been indeed remarkable shifts in attitude against the values of the
1960s — and for that matter, the 1950s and 1940s —
which suggest that we have now reached a historical
turning-point.

Obvious examples of this change of attitude can be found
in the now total rejection of the architectural tastes of the
1960s that gave us the urban high-rise blocks of flats and
littered our country with box-like dwellings of featureless less uniformity. In this respect, the change of taste is
surely to be welcomed. It is easy for the sophisticated to

make cheap fun in the press of people who buy their council houses and promptly trick them out with Georgian doors, brass knockers, curved fanlights, and reproduction stage-coach lamps; but reaction against what is drab and featureless in the architectural environment is surely healthy.

On a graver matter, the last few years have seen a revolution likely to be of a far-reaching kind in public thinking about education. The drift of thinking in the 1950s and 1960s, which gave us comprehensive schools and which encouraged educative curricula and techniques based on 'child-centred' laissez-faire principles, has suddenly been brought into question, and there is widespread talk of the need for wholesale reform of curriculum, approach, and basic philosophy.

There are parallel developments in other fields, bringing into question attitudes which have their roots even further back than the 1950s or 1960s. The Green Peace movement, the Friends of the Earth, enthusiasts for organically grown foodstuffs, and various conservationist bodies are compelling us to question afresh the effects of modern technology on the environment, on the food we eat, and on our health of body and mind. Pollution of the atmosphere by fossil fuels and by aerosol sprays, and pollution of the soil and its crops by chemical fertilisers and insecticides are being recognised as long-term threats to ourselves and to the earth we inhabit. The disaster at Chernobyl has cast a shadow over our technological expertise just when the incidence of AIDS (the 'moral Chernobyl' it has been called) has brought the sexual revolution grinding to a halt.

The Church is often criticised for being slow in catching up with changing attitudes in the secular world, and indeed nothing is worse than to see clergy and theologians hastening to be in with the latest trend. But when a great corrective revolution occurs, such as that which is now bringing a whole range of superstitions into question, then it behoves Christians to take notice. In this connection, a recent leaflet distributed late in 1986 by the Society of the Sacred Mission is illuminating. The Director of SSM laments that members of the generation he represents, with its roots in the 1960s, are made to look like 'middle-aged trendies' by the conservative young men now entering the community. 'Forgive me, brothers! But we have to learn to live together and understand one another. There is a renewed emphasis on prayer, on living the disciplined life, and a renewed interest in the traditional elements of the Religious Life, *viz* habit, Rule and Office.'

It seems to be a sign of the times that middle-aged people have to comfort one another in the face of the attachment of the young to discipline and tradition. Indeed, it is an unenviable situation to be locked in middle life by the attitudes of one's rebellious youth between a generation of old fogeys and a generation of young fogeys. But new developments in Christian thinking are producing just such a situation. *The Times* has recently reviewed the latest book by Hans Küng, the Roman Catholic theologian whose ecumenical enthusiasm for other faiths than Christianity made him a thorn in the side of the Vatican. He became an apostle of 'global ecumenical consciousness' who in the 1960s delighted liberal theologians anxious to free the Church from the fetters of traditional dogma and to hold Muslims and Buddhists in their embrace. What is interesting about the review of this book *Christianity and the World Religions*,[8] is the scathing attitude of the reviewer, Peter Ackroyd, and in particular his suspicion that Küng 'is imprisoned by his time — a time which is now passing' (*The Times*, January 8th, 1987).

This acute sense that we have passed into a new theological era more sympathetic to doctrinal clarity and traditional discipline is in line with the other changes. Theologians still hung up on the doctrinal and moral relativism of the 1960s are bound to seem anachronistic. Nothing has struck me more forcibly in my travels in the USA than the eagerness of young people in their twenties to question the drift of our civilisation, both in its technological and in its moral assumptions. Up to a point, the young will always and quite rightly question the values and the set-up handed on to them. But the questions of the contemporary young seem nowadays to have unexpected philosophical depth. A lecturer who addresses them finds that it is not a matter of facing students who demand what is the point of this restriction or that, this tradition or that, handed on from the past. It is a matter of facing students who are questioning the fundamental assumptions which have produced a world of such violent contrasts between ease and suffering, wealth and privation, where a moral free-for-all is rotting the social fabric of the nations in the materially prosperous West.

Nothing could be more cheering to the thoughtful Christian than this awakening among the young to challenge the validity of attitudes accepted during the last few decades. They are attitudes which have helped to hand on to them a world riddled with famine and disease, and permanently organised at immense expense, so that its civilisation and its inhabitants can at any moment be totally annihilated by the pressing of a button in Washington or Moscow.

Notes

1 Harry Blamires, *Where Do We Stand? An Examination of the Christian's Position in the Modern World* (Servant Books: Ann Arbor, Michigan, 1980. SPCK: London, 1980).

2 Harry Blamires, A Defence of Dogmatism (SPCK: London, 1965): in the USA as *The Tyranny of Time* (Morehouse-Barlow: New York, 1965).

3 Paul C Vitz, *Psychology as Religion: The Cult of Self-Worship* (William B Eerdmans: Grand Rapids, Michigan, 1977).

4 H A Williams, 'Theology and Self-Awareness', *Soundings: Essays Concerning Christian Understanding*, ed A R Vidler (Cambridge University Press: Cambridge, 1962).

5 H A Williams, *ibid*.

6 John Rae, *The Times* (January 13th, 1987).

7 P Williamson and K Perrotta (eds), *Christianity Confronts Modernity* (Servant Books: Ann Arbor, Michigan, 1981).

8 Hans Küng, *Christianity and the World Religions* (Collins: London, 1987).

5
The Christian World

The Christian Inheritance

Eric Mascall concludes his book *Grace and Glory* with an illuminating chapter, 'The Things That Are Not Shaken', in which he sums up 'the notes of Christian living which mark off the Church from the secularised community which surrounds it'.[1] He defines the essential characteristics of Christian life and Christian understanding by three terms, 'intensity', 'vastness', and 'permanence'. In the first place, Christians live 'with tremendous zest and concentration', immensely varied in their personalities and gifts, but sharing in common 'the intensity of the love which they bear towards God' and which is 'nothing less than God's own love, which he has communicated to them'. In the second place, the Christian escapes the 'constricted world of the secularised man, constricted in space, in time, and in human population'. For the Christian 'life stretches out beyond the grave into an eternity of unimaginable amplitude and richness; and the society to which the Christian belongs is not just of the handful of people whom he can meet on earth and from whom he must part almost as soon as he has met them, but embraces in its scope all God's servants from the world's creation to its final dissolution'. In the third place, the Christian transcends 'the transience and elusiveness, the fragility and fleetingness of even the best things that life can offer' with 'the assurance of the things that do not pass away'.

Intensity, vastness, permanence: this concise summary of the notes of the Christian inheritance represents both the promise of what is to be fully realised hereafter and a description of what we should be tasting here and now. When I first reflected on Dr Mascall's summary, I wanted to add a fourth note. St Thomas Aquinas defined the three essential requisites of beauty as *integritas*, *consonantia*, and *claritas*: 'wholeness', 'harmony', and 'radiance'. *Integritas* and *consonantia* together connote a relatedness of every facet to every other facet in whatever experience, presentation, or understanding is involved, and this also seems to me to be a peculiar mark of the Christian mind and the Christian life. But a careful reading of Dr Mascall indicates that what I am seeking to define thus is already comprehended for him in his use of the term 'intensity'. For he observes of the great Christian saints that all their activity is derived from 'contemplation of God himself in his infinite energy, love, and power'. And for this reason,

> the activity of the saints is not like the activity of so many people at the present day, sporadic and unco-ordinated, but is altogether coherent and concentrated into an irresistible stream of power, since it is nothing less than God's own power flowing out into the world through the concentrated lives of his servants.[2]

Not 'sporadic and unco-ordinated, but ... altogether coherent and concentrated'. Whether we need two terms or whether one will serve makes no matter for the purposes of the present argument. 'Intensity' and 'coherence' are essential notes of Christian living and Christian thinking. And as the thoughtful Christian surveys the current scene, and indeed the story of our century, he cannot but be aware that human experience, even the experience of professing Christians, is all too often marked by apathy and inertia which are the reverse of intensity and by discreteness and fragmentariness which are the reverse of coherence.

The activity of the saints, Dr Mascall tells us, is 'coherent' and 'concentrated'. The verb 'concentrate' means in the first place, 'to bring towards a common centre or focus'. It is closely related to the adjective 'concentric' which means 'having a common centre'. The coherence of the saint's activity is thus due to the fact that it is all focused on a single centre, namely God.

We find it difficult today to think of human experience thus interrelated by concentration on a single focus. Popular journalism will speak of a man's 'public' life and his 'private' life, or of his 'professional' life and his 'personal' life. Such expressions, harmless in themselves, tend to encourage us to think in terms of life divided into compartments. We learn to compartmentalise our world and our activities from our earliest days. School life, family life at home, leisure life outside the home — these are distinct compartments. And each has its subdivisions. As we move at school from a history lesson to a geography lesson, from a chemistry lesson to a French lesson, we become acquainted with a series of fields of thought and activity between which the only interrelating factor is either the school which lays on these experiences or ourselves who are conducted through them. Of course, as we mature, groupings define themselves. We recognise that going to the gymnasium or the swimming-bath or the sports field is a different category of activity from sitting in the classroom, that French and

German and Latin are linked together, and chemistry, physics, and biology are linked together. The educational train, as it were, moves forward, dragging its language and science and artistic compartments along, and we shuffle about along the corridors from one to another. There is a kind of structural unity about this machine which pulls us forward through time, be it likened to a train or to a conveyor belt, but the only other principle of unity lies in ourselves as pupils.

As we grow older, there is little to encourage us to shake off our habit of thinking of human activity in separate compartments. Our Sunday newspaper will sectionalise itself into Business pages and Sports pages, Foreign news pages and Home news pages, Gossip pages and Entertainments pages. From day to day we move between home life and office life or factory life, between social activities and recreational activities. When a theologian writes that the activity of the saints is coherent and concentrated because it is nothing less than God's own power flowing out into the world, we nod our heads in agreement and picture the saints almost permanently preoccupied with thumbing Bibles and missals, ever on their knees in devout meditation, perhaps distributing crumbs to birds and spare coats to tramps, or perhaps even sitting eccentrically atop of columns in profound stillness. There indeed is the power of God flowing out into the world, we may agree, but we privately suspect that it is not getting the world's work done and that for every saint who chooses to perch on top of a column there must be a few people like you and me who earn our living and keep the wheels of industry turning. In short, we compartmentalise sanctity into a professional specialism which is no doubt highly desirable, but rather parasitic nevertheless. What we never think of doing is to relate the theologian's teaching about the coherence and concentration of the saint's activity to our own daily wrestlings with the stock market, or with customers at the post office counter, or with expanding the firm's export markets. That, as we say today, is a different ball-game.

But then no more do you relate your daily efforts at the post office counter or on the Stock Exchange with the news that your wife is pregnant again. What connection could there possibly be between such matters, except that they pertain to you in their totally different categories? You learn today that government stocks are down and that your little girl has got measles, but you put on different hats for registering these pieces of information and for responding to them; indeed, the notion of any connection between them would surely be improper. If you are a church-going Christian, you recognise that there ought to be a connection between Jane's measles and your prayer life; but you would rightly shun the notion that the collapse of the stock market ought itself to be the subject of earnest prayer. 'To work is to pray' we are told, and we nod our heads knowingly as we picture a craftsman busy with some aesthetically satisfying workmanship. We don't picture jobbers or brokers waving bits of paper in the air and clamouring for more stock in the latest privatisation issue. (Perhaps it isn't really work at all. Perhaps, like other forms of gambling, it should come under 'Leisure Activities'.)

We are trying, by these perhaps extreme examples, to highlight the compartmentalisation of life and the difficulty of giving human activities in diverse areas any kind of overall coherence. The whole drift of contemporary attitudes is to try to locate whatever principle of unity life may have in the person of the experiencing subject. Life is conceived as eighteenth-century novelists such as Defoe and Smollett pictured it. There is no shape, no pattern to it. There is just the continuing presence of the hero persisting through all manner of diverse experiences. Other characters float in and out of the book. These belong to the hero's early days; as he grows older they are dismissed from the story and forgotten. These belong to his university days; as he leaves the university they are dismissed from the story and forgotten. These belong to the years of his Continental tour; as he returns home to settle down they are dismissed from the story and forgotten. So the story continues in what is called the picaresque novel, recording the hero's doings and treating all others as of no account except in so far as they impinge upon his career. He is the only principle of unity giving shape to the book.

Is human life like a picaresque novel in which the only principle of unity is the experiencing self? Or is it more like a play, planned and shaped by a dramatist who locks characters together in a pattern of action? It is not like a play in being plotted from beginning to end so that individual characters have no freedom to act as they wish. But it is certainly like a play in that there is a principle of unity given to it by its Creator. Long ago, I met a woman who had retired from a stage life in which she had performed leading soprano roles with the old D'Oyly Carte Opera Company. I do not know whether she had adopted an amusing affectation in order to tease people or to save herself the trouble of boring conversations, but if anyone talked to her about the Gilbert and Sullivan operas, mentioning some aria or ensemble, she would smile and say, 'I'm sorry. I don't know that bit. I was always off stage for that.' She said it in such a way as to convince, but we may doubt whether it was possible to learn, rehearse, and perform the part of Yum-Yum, say, and not to know the tunes sung by the Lord High Executioner when she is off stage. But if it were possible to perform lead parts in Gilbert and Sullivan operas and to remain ignorant of each opera as a whole, then perhaps here is an instance of how not to think of the work of either Gilbert or Sullivan. I was reminded of this lady's attitude recently when I saw a production of Sir John Vanbrugh's comedy *The Provok'd Wife*. It is a comedy with a complicated plot which ramifies into sub-plots. The company performing it was not quite big enough to assign a different actor to every minor part. One versatile young actor functioned successively as a Singing Master, a roistering gentleman, a Justice of the Peace, and a *valet de chambre*. What sense would Vanbrugh's play have had for him had he known nothing of what happened on stage between his various appearances? Suppose he had built his conception of the whole simply by assembling together the piecemeal fragments of action in which he was involved, regarding his personal role, or accumulation of roles, as the essential principle of unity giving pattern to the whole?

This is how we tend to look at life nowadays. The weaker the sense of a structured universe in which human beings have to play out their lives, the less likely it is that they will bear in mind obligations to any authority outside themselves. If the role of a human being is inevitably played out in an environment which is a random aggregate of fragmentarinesses, he or she will clearly have to find meaning and pattern within his or her own being. One reason for the decay in our time of respect for authority, of the sense of obligation to principles and codes, is precisely this loss of any sense of an earthly scene in which there is design and purpose, in which things may hang together irrespective of your participation or my participation in experiencing them. Anyone familiar with Elizabethan literature will realise that in other ages men and women have been more conscious of themselves as operating within a divinely ordered system where their activities might resonate with echoes from an answering environment. We have so lost this consciousness that we tend to foist on to literature of the past interpretations which are alien to the works in question. For instance, in Shakespeare's *King Lear* we have a finely designed study of what happens when the functioning of the hierarchically ordered universe is interfered with. The king must govern his subjects as the sun must rule the planets in the heavens. The kind of disaster which occurs when the planets wander in disorder matches the kind of disaster which overtakes a kingdom in which the king no longer rules. A king who abdicates, thinking that he can take a well-earned rest from responsibility, is opting out of his duty. A father who hands over his power to his children is defying the law of authority and responsibility in the little kingdom of the family as he has defied it in the larger kingdom of the state. And this is not the end of the correspondences which Shakespeare exploits. For as the sun must rule the planets and the king must rule his subjects, as the father must govern the offspring and age must govern youth, so within the microcosmic kingdom of the individual being the sovereign reason must govern the emotions and appetites which otherwise would wreak havoc with it. Thus Lear's abdication is an offence against order in the body of the universe itself, in the body politic, in the body domestic, and in the microcosmic human soul. The consequences are logically traced. Goneril and Regan, uncontrollable in their appetites, get a free run in the country. They become the tools of the villain Edmund, the symbol of lawlessness by his illegitimacy, the man who can declare, 'Thou, Nature, art my goddess: to thy law my services are bound'.[3] Indeed, the worship of Nature, as we have seen, is the only alternative to the worship of supernatural authority which alone can restrain and regulate it. Edmund's words are the same as Eve's before the rifled tree.

Shakespeare's symbolism makes no concessions to our tenderer susceptibilities in that it treats bastardy morally rather than psychologically. Bastardy is a condition symptomatic of lawlessness in that the institution of marriage has its place among the hierarchical structures by which Nature is tamed and regulated, human appetites governed, and civilisation forwarded. It is not a psychological question whether Gloucester ought to give his lawful son, Edgar, precedence over his illegitimate son, Edmund: it is a moral obligation. It is not a subtle psychological matter that the king abdicates: it is a sinful act of disobedience, flouting the very principles of order on which civilisation rests. It requires no great investigation to explain why Lear goes mad. His initial sin is an affront to reason, an abdication of reason. As Goneril and Regan ravage the civil kingdom, the uncontrolled passions ravage the kingdom of Lear's mind.

There is a good deal in this kind of thinking which the modern mind kicks against, and here is no intention to recommend that the clock of history be reversed and that we embrace discredited superstitions. Nevertheless, the medieval notions of the ordered universe which the Elizabethan age inherited certainly gave men and women a sense of participating in something more coherent than a succession of fragmentary experiences. The notion that the mixture of 'humours' which determined a person's disposition was related to the mix of elements in the outer world and that character and experience bore the stamp of planetary 'influence' was something which gave the individual a place in a cosmic drama, or rather a cosmic dance in which the inanimate world and all things living played their part. The spheres danced around the world, the planets danced, the earth danced between day and night, the elements danced — the air in speech and echo, breath and wind, the water in river and tide — the seasons danced, and in keeping with all this the princes and nobles of the world made their solemn dance like the stars in the heavens. War was a marching dance, a funeral a stately dance, marriage a joyous dance, and even the student's disciplines in music, arithmetic, geometry, and astronomy had their rhythmic measures. The awareness of a unified cosmos thus conceived reached out to embrace the progress of partners in loving, marrying, breeding, and dying.

Order in Creation

Human beings have always hungered after evidence of meaning and purpose in their world. They have always hungered after evidence of unity of design or significance in the seemingly discrete experiences that life offers them. This is how Shelley concluded a poem inspired by Jane Trelawny when she sang to the guitar one evening:

Though the sound overpowers,
Sing again, with your dear voice revealing
A tone
Of some world far from ours,
Where music and moonlight and feeling
Are one.[4]

A world 'where music and moonlight and feeling are one' is to the poet's mind a world 'far from ours'. But the Christian has no need to dream of a 'world far from ours' where what is here fragmentary and elusive will be unified and integrated. The kingdom of heaven is just such a world, and it is on offer here and now, within us and about us. We do not have to look out upon the good things of life — music and moonlight and love — and yearn that somehow, somewhere they may make sense together, may belong together; they do belong together. That is what the Christian doctrine of creation is all about. For a most inescapable aspect of the account of creation given in Genesis is the sheer orderliness of the process. There is nothing random or nebulous about it. We do not learn that God breathed one day upon the formless void and lo, there emerged a viscid semi-fluid, semi-transparent substance, the protoplasm. And God said: 'From among the elements thus varyingly combined in this unstable combination let vital properties emerge such that millions of years hence, if the one in a billion chance occurs, something may one day achieve vegetable, nay animal existence. And if perchance, millions of years later still, some hungry creatures should spend long hours stretching their necks upwards to feed on foliage wellnigh out of their reach, let their efforts be rewarded by the development of the genetic specification for a long neck. In brief, should such a remarkable concatenation of unforeseeable events occur, let there be no more of a to-do about it, but let there be a giraffe!' There is nothing vague or casual about the biblical account of creation. There is nothing suggestive of a massive historical role for the fortuitous. We do not learn that God looked down on the formless void some 10,000 million years ago and lo, under his very eyes, a dense primeval aggregate of matter at a temperature of millions of degrees exploded with a big bang, hurling expanding matter across the void. And God said: 'Amid the waves of particles travelling through space maybe matter will coalesce into stars and gas. With a bit of luck and the exercise of gravitation and much patience we might one day see discus-shaped structures developing with spiral arms. If so, well and good, let there be galaxies!'

No, the book of Genesis gives us a picture of creation as a planned, orderly, organised process. The sky and the land and the sea are made. Vegetable life is designed to produce seed and fruit. Birds and fish and beasts are fashioned. The whole procedure is organised, and it follows that what is was intended to be. No allowance seems to be made for delays of thousands of millions of years during which ambitious deer, weary of being fobbed off with what is obtainable on the lower branches of trees, may gradually extend their necks and turn into giraffes. There is something of a hit-and-miss air about the evolutionary developments that equip elephants with trunks and teach crabs to walk sideways. There is no hit-and-miss air about the biblical account of creation.

This point is not made in order to contrast the theory of evolution with the biblical account of creation as though the two were competing scientific explanations of how life began. They are not. Rather the point at issue here is that evolutionary theory encourages an outlook upon life which by its emphasis upon chance, graduality, and change, weakens our sense of the ultimate purposefulness of the universe we inhabit. By weakening

we need to preach that
the world is undergirded
but order + design, + unity of purpose

163

our sense of the purposefulness of life, it discourages
that awareness of the unity of design embracing our
world and our selves which Christian teaching insists
on. The Christian world is a world in which things fit together, in which things belong together. The doctrine of
divine creation emphasises that what we look out upon,
whether it is the galaxies and the regions of space, or the
mountains, rivers, and trees, is all purpose-built. Indeed, whether we look out upon the eyes and hands and
ears that make great works of art, or the brains that design computers and spacecraft, it is all purpose-built.
The order of creation is an integrated, unified whole. In
belonging to it we belong to a system, we might almost
say 'an institution'. We are not all cast abroad, lonely
and isolated, to fumble around for a role and an aim in an
alien environment teeming with manifestations of
evolutionary fortuitousness. It is the lack of a Christian
understanding of the world we live in that produces all
around us the shallow chatter of people lamenting that
they 'do not belong' and are 'seeking an identity'. We all
belong here as the stars belong in the sky and the bushes
in the garden and the tiger in the jungle. As for talk of
'seeking an identity', it is only another way of complain-
ing of a lack of a true sense of purpose, of a clear, defined
role and function. No child of God needs to go around
looking for an identity. No inhabitant of his created
world needs to talk of not belonging.

The realisation of our so-called 'identity', the appreciation of our human role is essentially dependent on
understanding the great drama in which we are called to
take part. The actor in *The Provok'd Wife* who performed in turn as a Singing Master, a roistering gentleman, a Justice of the Peace, and a *valet de chambre*,
would find no satisfaction in his successive roles unless

he appreciated the total pattern of action in which he was involved. You or I will fail in our successive roles unless we have the same understanding of the pattern of action in which life in time involves us. You can move between being a bureaucrat in the office, husband in the home, tennis player on the courts, fell walker at the weekend, taxpayer at the month-end, and sole owner of the vehicle registered B195 AFL at the year-end, but if you try to find the unifying factor in these successive performances simply in your own continuing identity throughout, you will find yourself on the road to despair. You may be part-time schoolteacher in the mornings, mother in the late afternoons, wife and cook in the evenings, Sunday-school teacher at the weekend, member of the Mothers' Union at the month-end, and registered claimant of full wife's earned income allowance for income tax purposes at the year-end, but if you try to find the unifying factor in these successive performances solely in your own continuing identity throughout, you will find yourself on the road to despair.

The Bible has something more than a doctrine of creation to give us our sense of participation in what matters eternally. The Bible records the cosmic drama of the Fall and redemption in which we are willy-nilly involved. There is perhaps too little teaching and preaching today which tirelessly extends our vision so that what we see about us we see in terms of the drama of the Fall and redemption. We have already stressed in this book how ubiquitous is the evidence around us of man's fallen condition, and how relevant therefore at every point in our response to our world is the realisation of sin and the knowledge that salvation is at hand. There is nothing in our experience which cannot be drawn by interpretation into due connection with the cosmic drama in which we take part. In my book, *The Marks of the Maker* (in the US published as *Words Made Flesh*), I drew attention to a passage in a sermon preached by John Donne in 1625. Donne takes up a current complaint that land is fetching a poor price. Was not land always very cheap? he asks. How cheaply did Adam sell the Garden of Eden, a very desirable estate, if ever there was one? How cheaply did Adam sell the human race? What price did he ask in selling immortality? Donne takes great pains to impress on his congregation what the sale of eternity amounted to. What is the value of a country manor, of a county, of a kingdom, or of the whole world, compared to what we sell when we trade our souls, our consciences, our future immortality, in exchange for a few grains of earthly dust which is all that we can possess here? We decry a man who sells a town or an army to the enemy; but Adam sold the whole world and its inhabitants — including Abraham and Isaac, Peter and Paul, evangelists and apostles; they were all sold by Adam; for Adam sold the whole race in advance. He even sold the Virgin Mary herself. Indeed, had not Christ been sinlessly conceived, he too would have been bartered away in advance.

The image of the human race sold into captivity under sin clearly appealed to Donne's imagination. He pictures sinners who sell themselves into the hands of the Devil by their taste for earthly possessions and lustful indulgences. Then he warns his congregation against thinking that they can wipe out the massive debt at the last moment before they die. A pirate may get away with it by bringing home his ill-gotten gains and bribing his way to a pardon. But you cannot bribe God in the last years of your life by endowing a hospital or leaving your money to some other good cause.[5]

Donne's sermon is cited because it shows how quick

Christians once were to move from the immediate scene and to cast their eyes over the whole sweep of human history from creation to redemption. It would be difficult for a member of Donne's congregation at Whitehall to leave the chapel wishing that he could belong. It might be easier and more tempting for him to leave the chapel wishing he did *not* belong, that his role in the human story were not so painfully apparent. Similarly, it would be difficult for a member of Donne's congregation to leave the chapel and muse on his lack of identity. His identity has been all too clearly declared. And identification which lays so substantial a weight of moral obligation and responsibility on the identified might be regarded by the unregenerate as a mixed blessing.

We are saying no more than that for the Christian, God is the centre of all things, his purpose and his way with mankind, the determining factor giving coherence to all that we are involved in. If Christianity were a less comprehensive, less thorough-going, less all-embracing religion, it would be more readily acceptable to our contemporaries. Christ as a great model and teacher: yes, that is widely accepted. The mystic experience and its healing effects: yes, that is widely understood. The call to universal brotherhood and to care for the sick and the afflicted: yes, that chimes in with the awakened social conscience of today. But divine creation, the Fall, the incarnation, the redemption, the kingdom of heaven: mix up all that with Christ the teacher, with the mystic experience, and with the social gospel, and our contemporaries turn away. It is not just that the overwhelming comprehensiveness of the Christian message eludes them, or repels them. It is that the comprehensive thing, the all-explaining thing is alien to the modern mind, nurtured as it is from nursery school days to ever-

continuing submergence in the piecemeal and the fragmentary. As Austin Farrer put it in his book *Saving Belief*:

> One of the chief difficulties a Christian meets
> in reasoning with unbelievers is that they do
> not see the whole evidence in that sweep
> which, to the eye of faith, is familiar land-
> scape. Isolating the physical creation, they in-
> sist on its brainless brutality, its opaqueness
> to any providential interpretation; isolating
> Christ, they insist on the preposterous singu-
> larity of the claims advanced on his behalf;
> isolating prayer or inspiration, the mystical
> fact, they insist on its queerness in a world
> which they wrongly suppose to be mere
> mechanism. But the Christian sees all the
> works of God, at every level, illuminated and
> supported by all the others in a graded sym-
> pathy. Christ, like the sun, casts light on every
> fact. Christ, like the sun, too bright to look
> upon, reveals his luminous power by the
> fresh colours he awakens in the wide garden
> of the world.[6]

Great Christian teachers have always allowed the
sense of the eternal to filter through to the temporal; they
have always seen the divine drama of redemption claiming men and women as participants at every moment of
their lives; they have always recognised the hand of God
at work in the daily presentation of choices and challenges on the human scene. This universalised view of
the individual human lot is what gives life its tremendous
significance. Allowing for the entry of God at all points
into human affairs turns the seemingly ephemeral eral

into the lastingly meaningful, the seemingly trivial into the momentous. The light of Christ, to use Austin Farrer's image, shines into the obscurest corners of our humdrum pedestrian doings to give them a brilliant prominence. Our slightest acts or decisions are picked out in the divine spotlight and projected in epic dimensions against the back-cloth of eternity. Thus it is in C S Lewis' *The Screwtape Letters*. The powers of hell and heaven bear down upon the question whether Wormwood's human patient is going to overcome his irritation at the way his mother lifts her eyebrow, upon the question whether he will take a country walk down to the old mill for tea. One day the young man reads a book for pleasure — without any ulterior motive of vanity or self-display — and takes a walk on his own simply because he enjoys it, and the senior devil comes down on the junior devil like a ton of bricks. Two solid but commonplace pleasures have been innocently enjoyed — without any intrusion of conceit or self-congratulation — and the diabolical progress to date against his soul is all undone. There is sorrow in hell and a hint of joy in heaven.

The understanding of life in terms such as these plainly overturns any scale of values based on worldly criteria. Christian insight allows the intensity and coherence proper to the truly beatific state to permeate the most humdrum experiences and draw them into a single pattern. The human issue may be only the question whether a young man controls his irritation at the way his mother raises his eyebrow, but the Christian ear detects in the distance the clash of angelic armies, the Christian nose scents at hand the snaking approach of a demonic tempter, and the Christian eye immediately magnifies the momentary into the momentous. The junction at which mood passes into mood or a choice of attitude is made turns out to be a parting of the ways to salvation or damnation. To use Dr Mascall's words, there can be nothing 'sporadic' or 'unco-ordinated' in even the minutiae of life lived thus in the context of salvation or damnation.

Christianity and Culture

But we must not allow imaginative intensity and rhetorical force brought to bear upon life's daily moral choices to blind us to the mellower aspects of life lived *sub specie aeternitatis*. Even Lewis' young convert spends innocent hours reading books and taking country walks. In tackling the moral aspects of that 'intensity' and 'coherence' that are proper to the Christian's daily pilgrimage, we have made his path seem thorny indeed. Similarly, in emphasising the fallen condition of the human race and its erosive effect on the body of our civilisation, animate and inanimate, we have tended to picture life as a demonically laid minefield. Yet you and I have only to cast our eyes around our neighbourhood to see evidence of the hand of God at work through our fellow-beings. There is a church spire rising above the local market town. There is a hospital long ago endowed by a local benefactor. There are schools which were initially established by Christian beneficence. There is a local chorus performing Bach's Mass in B Minor. There is an amateur dramatic group putting on Eliot's *Murder in the Cathedral*. In short, historically speaking, the environment is covered with the marks of past efforts to Christianise our culture and our civilisation. If we Christians sometimes feel lonely, few, and alien in our world, it may be partly because we have allowed our historical

sense to atrophy. For on the cultural scene our environment is alive with the rich products of our Christian inheritance, our Christian cathedrals, our Christian literature, our Christian art, and so much else. When the
Christian attends a performance of Handel's *Messiah* he
is 'at home' with the total event it represents. What does
the atheist feel, how does he respond, when he attends
such a performance, or when he studies the great artistic
masterpieces of Christian painting, Christian architecture, or Christian poetry? Does he say to himself, 'Well, I
simply cannot enter into this experience at all'? Does he
say, 'It's a pity I cannot share this artist's vision, a pity I
can never reach the heart of his inspiration, never
approach the core of what he seeks to convey'? Unfortunately, he says nothing of the kind. He does not even
think it matters. God forgive him, he thinks that the great
works of Christian culture are great *in spite* of their
Christian substance and inspiration and in no degree *because of* their Christian substance and inspiration.

This is how, at the cultural level, the world shields itself from Christian penetration. There is a sly pretence
that great Christian schools and hospitals, founded by
the faithful, have mattered simply because they are
schools and hospitals. In so far as they represented
Christian endeavour, that is quietly ignored and forgotten. There is a sly pretence that great Christian literature
and art, architecture and scholarship — the work of a
Dante or a Leonardo, a Wren or even a St Augustine —
has a cultural validity totally separable from the Christian context and the Christian inspiration. The very fact
that floods of atheists and agnostics pour annually
around our great cathedrals, indistinguishable from
those Christians for whom the places are houses of God,
devoted to prayer and worship, gives a kind of non-

Christian status to a specifically Christian artifact. In other words, we are deprived of our inheritance.

As another instance, consider how often you hear or read John Donne's words, 'No man is an island', quoted in such a way that their essential meaning is obliterated. For the context is totally ignored — the definition which the sentence illustrates. Donne insists that the unity which makes no man an island is the universality of the Church and its grafting of all men and women at baptism into the Body whose head is Christ. There is no hint in Donne of any sentimental notion of human togetherness apart from the Fatherhood of God, the Creator of all. Tearing Donne's words from their context, emptying them of their supernatural content, and using them to bolster sentiments which he would have derided is an instance of the secularist confiscation of Christian property which has become a feature of our culture. In similar fashion, literary scholars devote themselves to the study of *The Divine Comedy* and educate their students in appreciation of the work in such a way that whether an atheist is reading it as a fascinating construct of an outmoded mentality or a Christian is reading it as one of Christendom's great records of personal spiritual pilgrimage, is irrelevant to meaningful evaluation of the work. In the academic world especially our Christian inheritance is being filched from under our eyes.

Up to a point, there may be good in this. The more the secular world appreciates what Christianity has given to the world in the way of cultural works, the better, even though unbelievers enjoy these works with eyes closed to their specifically Christian significance. A cathedral packed with atheistical sightseers is surely preferable to an empty cathedral. *Paradise Lost* read is always better than *Paradise Lost* unread, whoever the reader. But the subtlety with which a wedge is driven between the Christian cultural inheritance and the body of Christians alive today is surely a diabolical subtlety. You will certainly not hear our secularised contemporaries say of you or me: 'Oh yes, he's a Christian. Like Bach and Milton, like Leonardo and Raphael, like the people who built our cathedrals and gave us our first schools: he's one of those'. Indeed, there is an attempt to isolate us from the very culture which is pre-eminently ours as Christians by playing down the Christian content of a work of art or literature as something which, if emphasised, would somehow vulgarise response to that work by sullying the purity of a supposed aesthetic substance loftily superior to creed or ideology. In this way, a movement is forwarded which seeks consciously to detach Christians from a culture increasingly in the hands of non-Christians. The active enemies of Christ want to push us out to sea in our ark of salvation, but first they are trying to empty our hold of everything other than specifically religious practices which Christian men and women have given to the world. They want to unload our freight at the dock-side. Then, having appropriated our cargo, they pretend that its Christian origin is an accident of history and its Christian substance a matter of mere packaging. They re-label it and trade it as secular merchandise.

We Christians need a conscious strategy in this matter. Personal commitment to our Lord in prayer and meditation and worship will alone supply the discipline on feeling and thought by which we can be directed aright at those junctions in the moral life of which we have spoken. But the intensity and coherence of Christian life lived in what Austin Farrer called the sunlight of Christ is not a matter of individual morality and individual spirituality practised in isolation from the current of civilised life. Indeed, it is because of the intensity and coherence of the Christian inspiration and the Christian vision granted to great artists as well as to great saints in the past that the impress of the faith lies upon so much in our culture; and in this respect, personal spiritual disciplines need to be supplemented by cultivation of an alert Christian cultural consciousness. We must take note of where the Christian impress lies upon our culture — whether it be in a book, or a painting, or an oratorio, or indeed in a work of mercy or philanthropy — and we must take care that it is known for what it is, and not allow the enemies of the Church to squeeze the juice of supernatural faith from its substance, so that what was once a genuine fruit of Christian inspiration is left looking like a dried-out skin. That is the positive corollary to much that has been said earlier in this book. We have taken great pains to identify where the Christian impress is totally lacking in our culture and our civilisation, where books and studies, projects and undertakings, are designed and conducted to counter any sense of man's affiliation to an order beyond time and space. We have seen where the forces of evil are at work in our midst. It is no less incumbent upon us to identify the fruits of Christian inspiration and endeavour for what they are, giving thanks for all that Christians have done in the past to enrich the lives we live today.

It ought to go without saying that there is a converse responsibility laid upon us to have nothing to do with the philistinism which has marred the record of some Christian bodies in the past. Members of the Christian Church which has produced the kind of artistic masterpieces we have referred to ought never to depreciate or undervalue, let alone to despise or condemn, those

things in the world of culture which not only enrich and
beautify human life, but also testify to the splendour and
power of the Creator who inspired their makers. It is
necessary to make this point in a book which has had a
good deal to say about the defects and follies of our
civilisation. There would be no point in making a fuss
about the state of our civilisation if all civilisation were
believed to be irremediably corrupt. Our concern for the
health of our civilisation arises out of the conviction that
in many respects it is, and in more respects it could be, a
wonderful testimony to what human hand and brain can
achieve when employed in obedience to God's will.
(You have only to check up among your own acquaintances to discover how many people, thanks to progress
in medical science, are today living active, pain-free
lives who have complaints which 60 years ago represented a death sentence — diabetes, glandular
deficiencies, and heart conditions among them.)

A key argument in this book is that counter-Christianity flourishes especially under two conditions which encourage it. The first is loss of the sense of emergency, of
life's precariousness, and of the pervasive power of evil,
which was analysed in Chapter 1. The second is loss of
the sense of that comprehensiveness of the Christian
faith which is the subject of this present chapter. The
first defect represents loss of proper awareness of human
need. The second defect represents loss of proper awareness of the Christian answer to that need in all its full-
ness. A true awareness of the all-salvaging character of
Christ's redemptive work will not stop short of seeing
whatever is good in the earth God made as hallowed, or
hallowable, when properly used. We live on God's earth,
made by him. We are God's creatures, redeemed by him
through the taking of our humanity upon him. We can-

not confine the significance either of the Incarnation or the Redemption within the limits of an ascetic spirituality and a puritan morality which are unresponsive to the magnificence of the created world and the splendour of what can be achieved by the human hand and the human brain.

It has to be accepted that there are Christians whose conversion has been an exclusively personal experience of surrender to Christ, initially untouched by intellectual or cultural implications. Such experiences, in the force of their immediacy, seem to require no validation from the record of history. But the Gospel itself is rooted in history and in the culture of the Jews. Even the most consciously born-again Christian will find sooner or later that personal commitment and personal evangelism cannot thrive in a vacuum from which intellectual and social problems are excluded. There are also Christians who like the present writer were overcome from the start by the comprehensiveness, the all-of-a-piece-ness, of what confronted them in the Christian faith. Here was a fabric of belief, philosophy, ethic, and practice which had stood the test of 2,000 years of history and which, if it were true, made sense of everything. Made sense of everything in that it alone answered such questions as: Who made the world? Why was it made? What are we here for? Why is human history such a mess? What is wrong with civilisation? What is wrong with man? Why should there be suffering as well as joy, cruelty as well as love, squalor as well as beauty? Why should there be a human consciousness to ask such questions anyway? What is it all about?

I speak as one who found in the Christian faith, as presented to me by teachers and writers, whether Protestant or Catholic, a strange unanimity in catering for the basic intellectual doubts that tease all thinking men and women, and an almost equal unanimity in prescribing codes of conduct which seemed to make sense in confronting the personal distresses and social ills from which we suffer.

Over and against the Christian view of life, what is there in which a thinking young man or woman can put their trust? What ideals can command confidence in the face of the realities of life facing us — the realities fully exemplified earlier in this book? In every decade of our century, trendy voices have invited us to throw off past superstitions and myths, and embrace the new promise opened up by scientific progress. The voices are heard, and they fade into silence. I seem to remember H G Wells beckoning us towards a rationalised, socialised, technological Utopia; Bernard Shaw preaching the word of the impersonal Life Force; E M Forster telling us only to 'connect' with each other in mutual emotional admiration, and all would be well. But has there ever been a decade in the twentieth century, with its massive wars and social upheavals, in which human behaviour and human prospects seriously matched up to the dreams of coming Utopias promised by optimistic progressives? Have we ever been in sight of that humanistic ideal where everyone lives in peace and brotherhood, egalitarian plenty, and cultured prosperity?

The crucial point here is that to me — as to so many other Christians who have had to determine their life's allegiances — the things in Christian teaching that fashionable eggheads airily dismiss as out of date have always seemed to be highly relevant and down-to-earth by comparison with the myths of the new humanism. Of course, we are incurable sinners. Of course, man is by nature prone to corruption, easily led into wickedness and folly, and can only by divine help hope to grapple with the ills around him. Life is plainly for many people a vale of tears. There are men and women all around us going through the 'valley of the shadow of death' (Ps 23:4), stricken by the 'arrow that flieth by day' or by the 'destruction that wasteth at noonday' (Ps 91:5, 6). The changes and chances of this fleeting world, with its wars and disasters, its undeserved diseases and afflictions, its bitter failures and disappointments, defy prudent men and women to set their hearts wholly on things below.

Christian teaching caters for the real and not for an imaginary world. Christianity can never be simply a matter of personal conversion determining the character of moral life. It is also a matter of intellectual enlightenment transforming the whole mental life. It is not only a matter of entering upon the life of spiritual regeneration, but of entering upon a total revaluation of all interests — intellectual, cultural, social, and personal — in the light of the Gospel revelation. And more than that, for much has happened since Christ rose from the dead. It is a matter of entering upon a vast inheritance of understanding and illumination shed over the whole created world and civilised life by generations of believers.

Notes

1 E L Mascall, *Grace and Glory* (The Faith Press: London, 1961; Morehouse-Barlow: New York, 1961).
2 E L Mascall, *ibid*.
3 William Shakespeare, *King Lear*, *The Works of Shakespeare* (Routledge, Warne and Routledge: London, 1864), Act I, Scene II (p62).

4 Percy Bysshe Shelley, 'To Jane: "The Keen Stars Were Twinkling"'. *The Complete Poetical Works of Percy Bysshe Shelley* (Oxford University Press: London, 1960), p673.
5 This summary of Donne's argument is reproduced from Harry Blamires, *The Marks of the Maker* (Kingsway Publications: Eastbourne, 1987) and *Words Made Flesh* (Servant Books: Ann Arbor, Michigan, 1985).
6 Austin Farrer, *Saving Belief: A Discussion of Essentials* (Hodder and Stoughton: London, 1964), p78–9.

6
The Christian Life

Progress in the Christian Life

We cannot get far in experiencing the life of the Church and the teaching of faithful priests and pastors without becoming more aware of the Pauline antithesis between meat and milk. Indeed, whenever we come upon an instance of heroic self-sacrifice by a man or a woman who has surrendered all earthly prospects for the sake of the Gospel, we are touched by a sense of admiration and then, turning our thoughts upon ourselves, we begin to measure the comparative feebleness of our own offering. We forget for a moment the difference between believers and unbelievers and focus instead on the difference between believers themselves. Let us examine this difference by analogy. Suppose you cannot play a musical instrument and you belong to a social or religious circle where the services of a pianist are often needed. You and all the other non-players are full of admiration and envy for the man or woman who can just sit down and play a tune for a dance, a song, or a hymn. The gap between you and all the piano players in the world seems a vast one indeed. You determine to bridge it. You practise hard and after two or three years you find yourself able to do exactly what those you envied could do when a song, or a dance, or a hymn is called for. But you also discover, to your chagrin perhaps, that the gap between you and those virtuosi who play piano sonatas and concertos on the radio is a far, far bigger gap than the gap between you and your non-playing friends who envy your progress. Suddenly the gap between the world's piano players and the non-players ceases to be the gap by which you measure your progress.

As an analogy of progress in the Christian life this has a certain usefulness. We become practising Christians, perhaps, out of a vague hunger for inner peace, and after a search for purpose and direction in our lives. We accept the need to go to church, we begin to read our Bibles, and to say daily prayers. We acquire a vague sense that our lives can be equipped with an additional dimension, that they can be enriched by something called spiritual experience, in fact, that everything we have previously been involved in can be freshly packaged in colourful wrappings impregnated with the odour of sanctity. Then we begin to listen to sermons or to read religious books, and a different note strikes our ear. There is a great deal of talk about surrendering our wills to God, about making God the centre of things in our lives—of all our aspirations, purposes, and reflections — about losing ourselves in Christ, allowing him to take us over. And the recipe for achieving this seems to involve obliterating all kinds of personal tastes and inclinations. We hear of people submitting themselves to programmes of prayer, meditation, fasting, and penance, all in the cause of the divine take-over. Suddenly, like the person who has learned to play the piano, we feel that the gap between ourselves and non-Christians is fading into insignificance. The gap between ourselves and — not just the saints, but the practised Christians we observe among our fellow-worshippers — seems a massive gap indeed.

If we are tempted to despair, there are messages to comfort us. We recall that though Mary was praised for having chosen the better part, Martha actually made the dinner that sustained the praiser and the praised. Moreover, St Paul has much to say about the multifarious variety of ways in which Christians can serve. There are diversities of gifts but the same Spirit. Of course, we must be careful not to treat this as an escape route: 'I'm the active type; I leave praying to others'; 'I'm the intellectual type; I leave the practical good works to others'.

I heard a bishop at a confirmation service exhorting the young confirmands to make some simple rule for ensuring that they kept a place for God in their lives. In a mood of seeming enthusiasm he praised a much-occupied businessman who had said, 'I always set aside seven minutes a day for God'. Perhaps in order to clinch his point and to get into the minds of the young confirmands the idea of making a commitment they could keep, this concrete example had its merits. But though it might be a starting-point for newly confirmed 12-year-olds, questions bristle about the age and experience of the businessman whose priorities and sense of proportion seemed to be cited with approval.

Yet clearly we cannot measure the fulfilment of our duties to God in man-hours, let alone man-minutes. Although the best guides to the spiritual life tend to recommend the making of rules for regular prayer and Bible study, yet equally all the best guides to the moral life tend to recommend the breaking of such rules when the call of human duty intervenes. A fireman must put his Bible down if he is called on duty. A mother could scarcely justify sticking to her 15-minute prayer schedule while her baby was screaming itself into hysteria and her aged parent was tottering around the house in search of aspirins. When guests visit us, we may find ourselves skipping religious duties in order to look after their comfort. If there are times when we forgo our private Bible study because we are going out to the theatre, there are also times when we forgo it because a garrulous visitor wants an attentive ear into which to pour his repetitive self-commiserations. In the former case, pleasure calls us from our duty and we feel guilty for having avoided a comparatively sombre obligation. In the latter case, sympathy, whether deserved or misplaced, calls us from our duty, and we think ourselves unlucky to have forgone an activity so comparatively tranquil and relaxing as meditating on God's Word.

Common sense is a most necessary guide to progress in the Christian life. One of the most notable marks of such progress will probably be the sheer lack of fuss, for this is what marks so much of what our Lord did. Granted that we cannot always be sure how far the attitudes and personal style of the evangelists affected the tone of their narration, the fact remains that our Lord's most remarkable acts were distinguished by this lack of fuss. Consider the account of the feeding of the 5,000. Or return again to the story of Zacchaeus. When our Lord went into Zacchaeus's house, some of the populace certainly seem to have made a fuss, but there is no record of any response by Christ in kind. Or consider the healing of the Centurion's servant. Something of a to-do was made in appealing to our Lord. In St Luke's version of events the elders of the Jews who brought the appeal had much to say about the Centurion's sympathy for the Jewish people and his generosity in building them a synagogue. But when our Lord actually set out for the Centurion's home, then the Centurion sent servants rushing to intercept him with the request that our Lord should stop short of visiting him.

> Lord ... I am not worthy that thou shouldst enter under my roof ... but say in a word, and my servant shall be healed. For I also am a man set under authority ... and I say unto one, Go, and he goeth; and to another, Come, and he cometh; and to my servant, Do this, and he doeth it. (Luke 7:6–9)

The significant thing is that, again in St Luke's version, our Lord turned round as soon as he received this message. The request for the absolute minimum of fuss seems to have chimed in with his own thinking. It is small wonder that our Lord then turned to those following him and said, 'I have not found so great faith, no, not in Israel' (Luke 7:9). But the rest of our Lord's response remains slightly surprising. We might have expected that when a great prophet received the message 'Lord, I am not worthy to receive you at my home', he might have shown his magnanimity and appreciation by going along there and rewarding the protester with the gracious honour of his presence. But the economy of demonstrativeness recommended by the Centurion seems to have weighed even more heavily than the confession of unworthiness. For this request to forgo all etiquette, all fuss, bespoke a directness of faith that shot like an arrow cleanly to its mark. 'Don't trouble to come here. Just say the word. It would have its effect as quickly as would my word if I ordered a soldier to saddle my horse.'

Now this simplicity and directness of dealing between our Lord and the Centurion somehow ought to mark the Christian's relationship with God. The fact that the Centurion's response—'Lord ... I am not worthy that thou shouldst enter under my roof ... but say in a word'—has been utilised in the liturgy indicates how meaty its implications are. But it is illuminating to lay emphasis on the other side of the interchange between the Centurion and Christ; the fact that our Lord immediately turned round and called off his proposed visit as completely unnecessary. The word can be spoken at a distance, the order given, and the patient healed.

Reflect what surely *might* have been the effect of this choice of action on our Lord's part. Surely, since Christ failed to turn up at the Centurion's house, the onlookers could with perfect reason say, 'Well, he didn't come; but the patient got better anyway. Obviously Jesus had nothing to do with it. If he *had* come, we should all have given him credit for a cure that was to happen anyway, shouldn't we? That's how supersititions grow'. The Centurion was himself a man of different calibre to that. Every word in his message to our Lord conveyed implicit trust, total trust in his power to heal the servant from a distance without any personal visitation. His faith was crystal-clear. 'I order a man to fetch my sandals and he fetches them. Jesus orders my servant to be healed, and he is healed.'

The sequence says something about the way in which prayer may be effective. If prayer is made in absolute trust, there will be no need for a personal public visitation making clear to all the neighbours that God has paid us a call and granted our request. The thing can be granted on the nod and we can all say, if we are so inclined, 'Well, he didn't put in an appearance, but I got what I wanted anyway, so probably prayer had nothing to do with it'.

The Need for Simplicity

Progress in the spiritual life will not necessarily be marked by ever more evident divine visitations. It appears that if our faith is sufficiently direct and unquestioning, our Lord will be able to turn back from approaching our home with a retinue and go to call on someone else instead. Likewise, progress in the spiritual life will not be marked by ever greater brilliance or complexity of achievement; and this is where the analogy with making progress in musical skill would break down. We hear that a great conductor can sing, 'God Save the Queen' while playing, 'Rule Britannia' with his left hand on the piano and conducting the opening of the 'Eroica' symphony with his right hand. The saint who has advanced far in the spiritual life will make no comparable boast that he can write out the first chapter of Genesis while mentally saying the Magnificat and orally reciting the Lord's Prayer.

There is more to be learned from the fact that our Lord did not visit the Centurion but gave the nod from a distance and the servant was healed. We tend to look for something more in response to our prayers than the fulfilment of our wish. We tend to look for some compulsive evidence that the fulfilment is the direct result of prayer. We make our prayerful requests month after month, year after year, for the health and safety of our loved ones, for the solution of this one's personal problem and that one's personal problem. The years pass and no great disasters overtake them or us, just the usual mixture of threats to health and happiness or life itself which mercifully are lifted before calamity strikes. We tend to wonder whether God has played any part at all in respect of the passing of those worries and threats about which we prayed. Everything that happened happened so naturally. A did arrive safely home from all those flights. B's trouble was not cancer after all. C did recover from the breakdown. D did not lose his job. Were we foolish to worry? Were we wasting our time in praying? Perhaps such questions do not occur to us. Even so, we find ourselves saying one day, 'I'm not the kind of person to have religious experiences. Oh yes, I say my prayers; but I'm never really aware of a divine response'. Then we check ourselves. What is A's safety, B's present health, C's recovery, and D's continuing employment but a divine response? No, we tell ourselves, that is making too much of what is a perfectly natural sequence of events. Anyway, we cannot believe ourselves so important in God's eyes that he would have thus immediately and actively responded to our request. We cannot believe that it is as simple as that. Besides, we prayed hard for E, and she died just the same.

What about the Centurion? He did not say, 'Lord, I am not worthy that thou shouldst fulfil my request on the nod'. He said, 'Lord, I am not worthy to receive a personal visit; but just say the word'. The word was all-important to him, the granting of the request, without any question of crowds of onlookers watching the Master descend upon the house to heal the sick with an authoritative word and a dignified gesture. No wonder our Lord said that he had not found so great faith in Israel. As for us, we pray daily for the safety of our loved ones, and perhaps none of them has yet been maimed or killed on the motorway. Yet we think to ourselves, 'I'm not the kind of person to have living experience of God, to sense his presence, to feel his touch'. We lack the Centurion's faith.

Certain questions seem never to have entered the Centurion's mind. One was: '*Can* this man heal my servant?' For him, the question would have been exactly on a par with 'Will a horse be put between the shafts if I order my men to prepare my chariot for the road?' Another question which seems not to have occurred to him was, 'If my servant does indeed get better, how shall I know whether this man has had anything to do with it?' On the contrary, the central emphasis of the Centurion's thinking seems to have been: 'In my realm of authority I don't have to move hand or foot to get things done even at a distance. I give the order and men set about their tasks wherever I have posted them. In this man's realm of authority the same law applies'.

Stories like this are too direct to allow us to read subtleties into them. Modern self-consciousness introduces psychological complexities into man's response to God which in biblical times seem to have been less intrusive. There is often a directness and simplicity of human purpose and response which we cannot but envy. Consider how the psalmist addresses God; how directly he praises God, then politely requests him to lay off, as we should say, to keep his temper, and deal friendlily with him. The psalmist will acknowledge his faults, will grovel in the dust with a request for mercy, but he will also stoutly protest his righteousness, demand fair treatment, and point out that some pretty repulsive types are getting away with murder. Mood succeeds to mood, and they are all moods we know well. But the frankness and directness of it have a blatancy which we half admire, half suspect. By contrast, we too often find ourselves plumbing layer below layer of motive, probing behind our own professions whether of trust or penitence. We tend to stop to ask: Am I being sincere? Do I really believe that? Though I feel like that today, shall I necessarily feel the same tomorrow? And we are tempted to query the very background of reality within which we operate, to ask: Am I just talking to myself? Is there anyone at all up there anyway? And if there is, is he the slightest bit interested? And why should I expect him to see anything in the same light as I see it?

Such questions, we know, ought not to arise; yet they come flooding into our minds today. They are the product of a high degree of self-consciousness, of subjectivity, and of scepticism which afflict the modern mind. This is what we mean when we say that the biblical record of God's dealings with his people and of their response to him defies any attempt to read subtleties into them. No doubt there is plenty in the Bible about human deception and trickery, hypocrisy and pretence; but the idiom of interchange between God and his people often contrasts sharply with modern habits of thinking which undercut professions of faith or purpose, requests or expressions of regret, by moving on to that lower layer of consciousness where questions flood in to complicate an issue: Is this profession, intention, request, or apology genuine? Is it sincere? Is it credible? Is it ephemeral? Is it disinterested? Is it based on wishful thinking? Does it conceal an ulterior motive? And if it is genuine, will it really appear so? The undercurrent of secondary brooding which subjects so much of our thought and utterance to sceptical scrutiny even as it is conceived or spoken is something we need to rise above. That is not to say that it is always a bad thing to analyse our own motives and to examine the sincerity of what we profess or purpose. But the habit of overlaying prayer and meditation with a mental blanket of cloud which shuts it off from the clear light of unself-conscious directness where yea means yea and nay means nay, and nothing more or less, where there are no accumulations of 'perhapses' and 'if sos', of 'maybes' and 'hopefullys' to shadow the terrain like the droplets of a mist—this habit is to be conquered. We have to acquire a simplicity and directness now foreign to our age.

The spiritual life of public worship, private prayer, Bible study, and meditation will flourish only in the clear atmosphere of simplicity and directness. This does not mean that there will be no complicated human problems to face, no tangled moral queries to tussle with. Making your spiritual life simple and direct will not magically transform your environment. It may be still as difficult for you to decide whether Mr X is a calculating hypocrite pretending to a faith he does not possess or an essentially vain, deluded fellow floundering in a sea of inconsistencies. But simplifying your own reflections may reveal how unnecessary it is for you to know the answer to that question anyway in order to pray for him.

How about the man who has just finished writing a religious book in which Christian orthodoxy is defended with abrasive rhetoric at the expense of those who dilute or distort the Gospel? How can he best crawl back from soap-box to altar in simplicity and directness of heart? Would it not be better to tear up the manuscript before begging for mercy? Would not that be the surest safeguard against diabolical pride?

I was once brooding on a question of this kind when I saw a remarkable piece of graffiti scrawled on a wall: 'Don't adjust your mind. There's a fault in reality.' Here indeed was a slogan calculated to shake the confidence of anyone who feels at odds with things as they are. If you believe passionately in a cause which most other people ignore, you will naturally be sensitive to the taunt: 'They're all out of step but you.' The Christian is bound to be out of step with much in contemporary life that bypasses religion. What if he also feels out of step with a good deal that is being said by fellow-Christians, with a good deal that is happening in the church of his baptism? Suppose he finds himself sometimes squirming in disagreement as he reads what bishops or theologians are saying? Is not such a situation an occasion for checking up on his own Christian commitment rather than for rushing into print to let off steam?

Self-examination on this question will present a man with two alternatives. Either he must turn on himself in mockery: 'Almost everyone is out of step but you. Don't adjust your mind. There's a fault in reality.' Or else he must seek the very dangerous consolation that truth-speakers have all too often found no sympathetic hearing in their own generation, and that the Christian's vocation to stand against 'the world' may sometimes involve apparently standing against 'the Church' in so far as it allies itself treacherously with the world. St Athanasius had to flee for his life to the desert. If the stories handed down are reliable, then he lived for a long while hidden in a dry cistern like someone holed up out of reach of a totalitarian secret police.

But surely, says the manual of guidance, surely this train of thought is spiritually most perilous. Surely the Devil would like best of all to persuade the man who is critical of the way things are going in Christendom that he's a modern Athanasius; that in the name of truth he must resist the tide of fashion! What more cunning method could there be of ensnaring a human soul with pride?

Well, actually, there *is* a more cunning method of ensnaring a human soul. And that is by persuading a man that taking a stand against falsehood or corruption is self-righteous, bigoted, and intolerant; that in the name of Christian love he must bend to the wind of fashion.

We seem to be on the horns of a dilemma. We Christians often are. The sequence of thought we have traced is a specimen of agonising too much over motives instead of getting on with the task in hand. There was a young lady who objected to the 10 Commandments on the grounds that they don't tell you what to do, and they put ideas into your head. She certainly had a point. The negative business of strenuously trying to prove that, whatever we do, we remain human sinners is surely redundant. There is something conceited about feeling the need to establish a point so obvious.

I have already quoted Djuna Barnes' words: 'Let go hell, and your fall will be broken by the roof of heaven.' An aspect of the Christian vocation is surely that we must be ready to accept the totally undeserved status of brothers and sisters in Christ promised us. An inheritance so inappropriate to our characters seems to issue from an almost grotesque divine overestimate of us. How can we fitly respond when we hear ourselves proclaimed joint heirs with Christ? Surely politeness requires us to protest a little: 'Oh no, no. Please. You're far too kind. I couldn't possibly. I'm a very ordinary person really. Another time perhaps.'

Any kind of resistance to God is pride. It may be more blessed to give than to receive, but so far as God is concerned, human beings have to be content for the most part to be on the receiving end. Even when, in church, the impossible assumption seems to be in the air that we are capable of putting on the whole armour of God and standing against all the wiles and assaults of the Devil, even then we have the right to marvel at the magnitude of God's grace, but we have no right to beg to be excused.

'Draw nigh to God, and he will draw nigh to you. Cleanse your hands, ye sinners; and purify your hearts, ye double minded' (James 4:8). We perhaps know a good deal more about double-mindedness than St James did. If there are occasions when biblical onslaughts on sin tend to leave us feeling comfortable in that the offences condemned are not offences to which we are prone, St James' words here leave us in no such comfortable immunity. Purity of heart is more likely to be the last than the first virtue we acquire — if we ever succeed in acquiring it at all. We are enmeshed mentally in such a tangle of motivations and purposes, worthy and worthless, that singleness of purpose is bound to elude us. It is the pure in heart who will see God, our Lord himself insisted, and Kierkegaard once preached eloquently on the theme, 'Purity of heart is to will one thing', showing how the heart slides away to this preference and to that from the single obligatory purpose of loving God above all else and expressing that love in everything we do.

If we follow any theme of Christian teaching to its logical conclusion, we shall come upon some formulation such as that, which is difficult to swallow — 'the single obligatory purpose of loving God above all else and expressing that love in everything we do'. It is difficult to swallow because it is meat and not milk, and our throats prefer something smoother. But such conclusions are not hard to swallow in the sense that elaborate arguments or subtle theories are hard to swallow. God's instructions are never hard to swallow because they are complicated. They are hard to swallow because they are so terrifyingly simple, so blindingly direct.

The healthy human throat is not too delicate for the task. When experts answered questions about cancer in a recent radio phone-in programme, a man who had had a malignant growth in the throat destroyed by radiotherapy complained that he was not yet able to masticate solid foods painlessly. It was explained to him that the cauterisation of the cancerous cells inevitably burned healthy tissues too. He would have to be content for some time to take plenty of gravy and liquids, and even to use a spray to correct the deficiency in saliva. 'Milk, not meat' appeared to be the regimen. But when the effects of the removal of the malignancy by fire have been softened by the healing touch of time, he will find that he can relish the solider foods so necessary to his return to full health and vigour. The analogy comes too conveniently to hand to be resisted. We choke spiritually when the insidious cells of evil multiply in our throats. There is only one therapy to destroy malignancy, the therapy of fire, the burning fire of penitence. The cauterisation will leave our gullets parched and sore, yet hungry for nourishment. By all means, let us soothe our throats on the consolatory milk of the Word which speaks of divine compassion and the hope of heaven. But if we are to return to healthy and vigorous participation in God's work, we shall need to try to masticate, however uncomfortably, that meat of the Word which yields its juice only when we bite hard into its toughness. It is the red meat whose protein strengthens us to confront with reasoned faith the massive fatuities and wickednesses of our world and the sly weaknesses of our own hearts.